Routledge Revivals

Mental Readjustment

Mental Readjustment

Sidonie Reiss

Routledge Revivals
Routledge
Taylor & Francis Group

First published in 1949 by George Allen & Unwin Ltd

This edition first published in 2018 by Routledge
2 Park Square, Milton Park, Abingdon, Oxon, OX14 4RN
and by Routledge
711 Third Avenue, New York, NY 10017

Routledge is an imprint of the Taylor & Francis Group, an informa business

A Library of Congress record exists under ISBN: 50000474

ISBN 13: 978-1-138-60160-4 (hbk)
ISBN 13: 978-0-429-46260-3 (ebk)

SIDONIE REISS

MENTAL READJUSTMENT

PREFATORY NOTE BY

ALEXANDRA ADLER, M.D.

LONDON
GEORGE ALLEN & UNWIN LTD
RUSKIN HOUSE MUSEUM STREET

FIRST PUBLISHED IN 1949

Translated from the original German typescript
"Lebenseinstellung und Lebensumstellung"
by Bernard Miall

PRINTED IN GREAT BRITAIN
in 12pt. Baskerville type
BY BRADFORD & DICKENS, LONDON, W.C. I

FOREWORD

LIFE is no longer regarded with reverence. All that was great, precious, and sublime seems to have vanished; the voice of humanity is silenced. A world has collapsed; and humanity stands bewildered before its fragments.

But something new *must* emerge from change. Above all, a new human being! What are we to do—where are we to go?

Individual-psychology, the doctrine of the Viennese neurologist and psychologist, Dr. Alfred Adler, offers a solution.

As a scientific system, of service in all departments of life, it is, in respect of the life of the ordinary human being, an invaluable means of orientation; but it is in psychotherapy and pedagogy that it finds its original and most essential application.

Yet it has a very special value for the men and women of to-day, because its philosophical content was perfected in accordance with the experience of the first world war, and because its truth and its necessity have been confirmed by nothing so much as by the latest and most terrible chapter of history, in which the whole human race was condemned to common participation and suffering.

To-day, then, a special and lasting emphasis should be laid on the fundamental note of Adler's doctrine: that the world cannot be saved by hostility, violence, and striving for power, but rather that mutual understanding, co-operation and confederation can satisfy the claims of the individual and make for the progress of the community. How this humanism is rooted and elaborated in a scientific system is explained in the theoretical section of this book, which deals with the fundamentals of the doctrine and its pedagogical indications.

The cases so thoroughly described in the practical section illustrate the practical application of the theory in therapeutical pedagogy and psychotherapy.

INTRODUCTION

We human beings have always been conscious of a desire to attain to a 'true,' or normal, or valid form of life; we want, that is, to give our lives meaning and direction; we want to live a full and satisfying life, in harmony with our own natures and with our fellow-men. Yet, although so many have sought to attain to this art of shaping our lives, to do so has always been granted only to a few, for this problem has always been one of the most difficult of human problems, even for persons living in peaceful and normal times, to say nothing of all those who find themselves amidst the chaos of the modern world.

Why, in the past, have so many sought to prove that it is so hard a thing to give one's life the form which is recognized as 'true,' or 'normal'? Was it not often said that the realization of such a desire was merely Utopian? Was it not even argued that human beings, by reason of their physical constitution, are exposed to cosmic currents, and subject to tensions, which are bound to disturb even our spiritual equilibrium? Was it not believed that certain innate tendencies were bound to disturb our inner harmony? And that the demands of everyday life, of one's trade or profession, and one's obligations to one's fellow-mortals, were too exacting to permit of peace and equanimity?

And if we examine the essential content of all these questions, one thing emerges clearly: that in all these objections one idea has to be dealt with, namely the notion that wherever man lives and has his being, wherever he labours and creates, he lives in a community of which he is a member, and that his existence, the development of his faculties, and the moulding of his life, in a psychic or spiritual as well as in a material, physical, practical manner, are very largely dependent on the extent to which he is able to take into account the facts of social or communal life; in other words, on the extent of his knowledge of human nature, and his ability to act in accordance with such knowledge.

There have always been talented individuals who have had more knowledge of human nature than their contemporaries. Now, it is a remarkable phenomenon that to-day so many people should believe that they understand human nature, while in fact the great majority know very little about it. How else would it be possible that human beings should feel so alien to one another, should be unable to find points of mutual contact, should seem incapable of understanding one another, not only in the great society of national communities, not only within the spacious compass of society, but even in the restricted circle of the family? Husband and wife, who believed that they knew each other thoroughly, are suddenly disconcerted by the monstrous possibilities of mutual incomprehension; parents are unable to understand their children; brothers and sisters know nothing of one another; friends find that they have no common language.

What do we really mean by knowledge of human nature? The ability to recognize the true countenance of a human being, his essential being, under the greatest variety of outward forms, and often behind veils and masks; to recognize it in all its manifestations, and to draw the relevant conclusions. And all efforts to give a more harmonious shape to the communal life of humanity, in individuals and nations alike, will be crowned with success only if, among other premises, what hitherto the individual has attained by intuition becomes a general possession—if the knowledge of human nature is practically taught, learned, and acted upon.

For a first and significant step in this direction we have to thank the individual-psychology of Alfred Adler.

Adler was a physician and neurologist who perceived the necessity of penetrating into the psychic life of the patient, and understanding it, in order to help him.

After he had spent some years within the orbit of his

eminent predecessor, Dr. Sigmund Freud, the brilliant founder of the science of psycho-analysis (he was never a pupil of Freud's, as has so often been erroneously stated [1]), any further co-operation of the two pioneers was seen to be impossible. It is not our purpose, in these pages, to elucidate the differences between Freud and Adler, but merely to write an introduction to the doctrine of individual-psychology. We shall therefore confine ourselves to the brief intimation that Adler was no longer able to accept Freud's conclusions, but, on the strength of new discoveries, had to go his own way.

Freud sees the prime cause of all psychic abnormalities and morbidities in the repression of instincts and instinctual conflicts, wherein the sexual instinct plays the leading part, and he seeks to effect a cure by making the patient conscious of the conflict, and by the sublimation of the instinct—that is, its application to culturally higher aims.

Adler, on the other hand, refers all psychic difficulties and disorders to a false orientation of the whole personality, to an erroneous attitude to life, and seeks to cure the patient by a readjustment of the whole personality, and therewith a transformation of all intellectual, spiritual, and characteristic manifestations. Thus, proceeding from a different fundamental conception, Adler, through many years of observation of difficult and nervous patients, suffering from all sorts of psychic abnormalities, was able to draw conclusions relating to the normal psychic life. He discovered laws which are valid for all psychic life—laws which are merely manifested in a cruder form in psychic disorders and maladies than in normal cases—and which indicated the course to be followed, not only in order to effect a cure, but —what is of even greater importance and value—in order to avert and prevent such manifestations.

As a psychiatrist Adler began, originally, by restoring to health by means of therapy (curative treatment) those patients who had deviated into psychic maladies. On

[1] See Hertha Orgler, *Alfred Adler, the Man and his Work*.

examining the subject more profoundly he discovered a way of preventing aberrations, and by prophylactic measures he facilitated a positive and uninhibited development of the patient's latent energies. His psychology, therefore, set itself a twofold aim: its purpose was to heal, and to build up.

As a psychology, Adler's doctrine disregarded the traditional standards of value; it took no account of ethics, morality, and custom. It had only *one* point of view, one line of orientation: that of general expediency—of service to the community. And so it became a pedagogic and social psychology, whose self-imposed task was: to heal, to build up, to educate, for the benefit—in a progressive sense—of the human community.

We shall now indicate and elucidate the basic ideas of the 'individual-psychology,' and at the same time trace the path which Adler followed in building up his scientific system.

CONTENTS

	page
FOREWORD	5
INTRODUCTION	7

THEORY

Chapter I	15
Chapter II	26
Chapter III	35
Chapter IV	43
Chapter V	47
Chapter VI	58

PRACTICE

I.	*A Child who falls on her knees*	69
II.	*The Silent Child*	81
III.	*A Case of Play-Therapy*	97
IV.	*"I can't get up in the morning"*	112
V.	*Two Anxiety-Neuroses*	116
VI.	*The Problem of the Application of Individual-psychological Therapy*	147

PREFATORY NOTE

SIDONIE REISS's book consists of two parts. The first gives the reader a summary of the theories of Alfred Adler's Individual Psychology and can thus serve as an introduction to this field. The second part presents a selection of fascinating case histories, which are followed through the various steps of adjustment during guidance.

Some of these cases would at the start have appeared unpromising to anyone undertaking to readjust them. It is therefore encouraging to read these reports. They give an indication of what can be achieved by skilful guidance. On the other hand, the book undoubtedly raises questions to which we do not as yet have answers. For instance, there is the question of failures in re-education : what causes them, how can one foresee and prevent them? The author avoids sweeping statements and nowhere does she try to give the impression that all cases will follow so successful a course as the fortunate ones described in this book.

It is evident that in Miss Reiss's work with people there is no nervous haste when progress slows up, no impatience or despair, even when the client is in a seemingly desperate state. Through all the discussions and other steps taken a line is followed which indicates that the author is always aware of the direction in which she is trying to lead her client and how far he can go. It is her confidence which seems to stimulate him in the end to adopt the author's positive and constructive outlook, and which promotes his adjustment to life.

Mental Readjustment will interest anyone who deals with neuroses and with problems of adjustment in children and adults. It is written in non-technical terms and, for this reason, should appeal to non-medical counsellors, teachers, psychiatric social workers and related professions.

Sidonie Reiss has had wide experience in the field of guidance, both in Europe and now in the United States. This forms a solid foundation upon which her approach—and undoubtedly her success—rests. Hers is not any shallow pat-on-the-shoulder technique. Her work has its basis in a profound philosophy of "Love your neighbour" which characterizes her approach, a philosophy that all through the ages of mankind has raised its voice again and again, only to be hushed repeatedly in human fratricide.

This book is another offer to the troubled world; to all those who feel challenged to study, and to try to redirect, both the disturbed mind of the individual and the misguided behaviour of groups.

ALEXANDRA ADLER, M.D.

New York City, 1948

THEORY

CHAPTER I

'INDIVIDUAL-PSYCHOLOGY' means: the doctrine of the psyche of the individual. A man is an individual; which does not mean merely that he is a single person, in contrast to the community; but Adler understands by an *in-dividuum* (Latin, individuus, a, um), an undivided personality, a whole, a totality of body and soul.

Every living organism constitutes a self-contained unity; by which, indeed, it is distinguished from dead matter, which can be dissected and divided into portions without losing any of its qualities. The living organism cannot be divided without losing its essential quality, its life. Life cannot remain static; it moves and strives. The living organism, the human being, which we are here considering, is composed of manifold organs and functions (physical and mental), which are all in movement, but which are purposefully directed. What determines the direction which they follow?

It is to Adler that we owe the discovery that this direction proceeds from the *individual,* the whole, the totality, to which every organic, physical function and every psychic action is subordinated.

> Two men, rambling amidst the mountains, are surprised by a violent storm. One of them enjoys the wonderful spectacle; he is conscious of the tension and discharge of the forces of Nature; he feels enriched by this experience, and is aware of an urge toward creative activity. The fundamental theme of a symphony takes shape in his mind—he is an artist, a musician.
>
> The other is exasperated by the storm and the waste of time which it involves. His vacation will soon be ended; his journey has cost him a great deal of money, and he has got nothing out of it. Moreover, he is nervous; what, he thinks, would his family feel if he were struck by lightning and killed?

However, he is comforted by the timely recollection of the fact that he has insured his life for a considerable sum, so that people would be bound to realize what a reliable, provident husband and father he was.

Two men: one has the artist's temperament, the other has the sober, anxious mentality of the business man. Precisely the same experience has affected two different men in a wholly different way. What is the explanation? It is because each man is following an entirely different course of life, which *unconsciously* influences his thoughts, his feelings, his desires, his actions.

Adler has realized that the intellectual and spiritual attitude of a human being, in short, what we describe as his personality, must be envisaged as a purposefully directed unity. Proceeding from this fundamental standpoint, he sees clearly that neither a single transaction nor any partial manifestation of the psychic life can lead to an essential understanding of a human personality unless one considers it in connexion with the total personality of the subject.

A highly successful merchant was regarded with the greatest respect and esteem on account of his intelligence, amiability, and magnanimity. He was a fascinating companion, and if any friend of his needed his advice or help he was always most ready to give it. If a collection was made for some charitable purpose, or if any social activity was to be organized, his name always headed the list.

As a wholesale merchant he had many foreign connexions, and on each of his journeys abroad it would happen that he would engage in an intimate conversation with any little clerk or employee, whether in the sleeping-car or in his hotel, and would question him concerning his circumstances. It always emerged, on such occasions, that the man was dissatisfied with his work and with his financial situation. The merchant would then give the man his address, saying: "If you are ever in my neighbourhood, look me up, and I'll see what I can do for you."

In short, he was what a man ought to be—full of interest,

and thoroughly social in his attitude. And if one of these people really came to him—as did sometimes happen—he would have to spend hours in a waiting-room, only to be sent away and told to call another day, when the same thing would happen; he would be unable to obtain an interview. As regards his own employees, this man exploited their time and their energies in the worst and most ruthless fashion; meanly avaricious, he haggled over every farthing. In his own family he was dreaded as a despotic tyrant. Can this be the same man of whom we were speaking? Here, surely, are contrasts which cannot be brought into harmony. But individual-psychology has no difficulty in solving the problem. This man has only *one* endeavour: he must always be 'on top.' In one department of his life he attains his desire by amiability, charm, helpfulness and generosity; in the other, by ruthlessness, exploitation and tyranny.

Thus, if we wish to grasp the personality of a human being, it is not enough to consider a single transaction, a partial manifestation. One can understand him only if one builds up a composite portrait, through observation and the combination of details; if one studies him in his bearing, his conduct, his dealings with his fellows, and his aim in life; if one knows his plans, his recollections, his dreams and fantasies. Adler has found that if the portrait appears to be complete in every respect, the unity of the personality *must* emerge from it, and that then the purposefulness of this unity must be plainly manifested.

Every man's life proceeds in a perfectly definite direction, towards a goal which *unconsciously* directs his thoughts, emotions, desires and actions. Every event, every experience, is accepted and elaborated with reference to this aim. In this context the expression: "A person *makes* his experiences" receives a special meaning. He makes, i.e. he causes and shapes them, in accordance with his aim.

On the basis of his observations, Adler assumes that the line upon which a man builds up his life lays itself down in very early childhood, and that in its fundamental structure it is already determined by the third, fourth or fifth year. He speaks of the guiding line, the plan of life, the form, the style of life, or the individual law of motion, or dynamic law, which amounts to the same thing; by the guiding image, or *finale* (final aim) he means the goal of unconscious striving.

Now, how does it happen that one man follows this path in life, and another, that? What is the origin of the plan of life, or the individual law of motion?

Adler the physician, proceeding on biological lines, reverts to well-known facts of organic inferiority.

In this connexion an inferior organ is an organ which is diseased, or enfeebled, inhibited in its growth, or retarded in its development; at all events, not entirely equal to its functions. This retarded development need not involve the whole organ; it may affect only individual parts of the organ; perhaps only isolated complexes of cells or tissues. It can even be so insignificant that the owner of the organ is not conscious of its inadequacy; or it may amount only to great sensitiveness, or excessive susceptibility. However, the slightest functional derangement is bound to affect the internal harmony of the organism.

Adler, then, proceeds from the long recognized fact that an inadequate organ can spontaneously effect a compensatory adjustment by additional effort, increased performance, practice, and training. A weak heart, for example, by suitable training, can be so far improved that its functions are completely restored.

An inadequate organ may be supported by the symmetrical organ; for example, if the hearing of one ear is imperfect the other ear can gradually so accommodate itself that the functional defect is very largely corrected. In certain cases of kidney disease one kidney may be excised, and the patient can be restored to perfect health if the remaining kidney is able to take over the functions of the one removed. An inadequate organ may be supported by another organ: with the amputation of one limb, other limbs may succeed in replacing it after practice and training. Here is an example: Hermann Unthan,[1] who was born without arms (so that here we have a case of inadequacy in the highest degree), trained his legs and feet until they were able completely to replace the missing hands and arms.

Again, one of the senses may come to the help of an inadequate organ; if the sight is imperfect it may find support in an enhancement of the sense of touch or of smell.

We call this kind of accommodation or adjustment a *compensation.*

If the effort of adjustment is particularly great there may be over-adjustment or over-compensation. Naturally, a favourable adjustment, a successful compensation, is possible only in so far as the organism as a whole is able and ready to take over the additional task. This readiness, as we are speaking of the physical and psychic totality, must be psychological as well as physical; it may even be the case that organic insufficiencies are compensated or over-compensated by purely psychical efforts.

For example, defective vision may be compensated by an enhanced visual psyche: that is, an enhanced internal faculty of perception, which manifests itself in a vigorous and concrete mode of thought, or in phantasy (cf. Homer, the blind seer).

Despite defective hearing, valuable achievements in the region of acoustics are possible (e.g. Robert Franz, Smetana, Beethoven, who suffered from deafness, or even became completely deaf).

In this connexion one may recall Demosthenes, who, despite—or even because of—his stammering, became the greatest of Grecian orators; or Camille Desmoulins, the great orator of the French Revolution, who suffered from a lisp. Although there is a certain difference between the former cases and the latter, inasmuch as in the former the compensatory efforts evoked by inadequate organs were

[1] *The Armless Fiddler: a Pediscript,* C. H. Unthan, George Allen & Unwin.

unconscious, whereas in the latter results were obtained by conscious and deliberate practice, yet one thing is common to all: the tendency to compensatory adjustment, and—which is more essential—the possibility and existence of compensation and over-compensation.

In the light of these facts, cultural achievements of the highest value may very often—though not indeed always—be regarded as the over-compensation of organic inadequacy.

All the cases hitherto cited were instances of successful compensation, of fortunate adjustment. But there are many cases in which the total organism is not capable of effecting a positive compensation; and these are, for our purpose, actually the more interesting, as they provided Adler with the basis of his doctrine.

There are even such cases of a purely organic nature. We have already seen that a weak heart can be restored to normal functioning by suitable training. But if the demand made upon the enfeebled organ is too great it may have a paralysing effect upon the function, and may seriously damage the whole organism.

Adler found that the same law of compensation which—as we have seen—was already known to operate in the organic world, was valid also for the psychic world; that the psychic life strives to overcome obstacles and to achieve perfection. He observed and studied the behaviour of backward children and refractory adults—of nervous and mentally ailing persons. He traced it back to its first origins, and always found the first beginnings of deviation in very early childhood. In these researches he found a number of factors which, although they did not necessarily determine the development of the child, nevertheless guided or misguided him into following a completely individual path. As such influential factors—which may operate in various combinations—he distinguishes:

1. Constitutional weaknesses and organic insufficiencies,

among which may be counted fractures, excessive ugliness, or other conspicuous characteristics;

2. An over-indulgent or 'mollycoddle' education.
3. An excessively strict or loveless education.
4. Unfavourable family circumstances.
5. Oppressive social conditions.

On the basis of his many years of experience of neurotic patients, Adler learnt to perceive and understand all psychic aberrations, all social types of behaviour, as unsuccessful attempts at compensation, unsuccessful attempts to overcome a condition of weakness, menace, and oppression, to escape from a position of inferiority, to emerge from a minus into a plus situation.

A child is born with an organic defect which does not readily admit of compensation. The functional inadequacy is evident from its earliest days. The child experiences—of course, unconsciously—the insufficiency of its defective organ, and has a feeling of extreme insecurity; its very existence is threatened. For example, a defective digestive canal gives rise, from the very first, to sensory disturbances which weaken the organism and make it less capable of coping with the difficulties attending all—even normal—development. Such a child has more difficulty in passing through the various phases of weaning, teething, learning to be clean, learning to walk and to speak; the organism is feeble, and there is a constant recurrence of acute physical symptoms.

When the child reaches the stage of 'discovering its ego,' when it begins to observe, to compare, and to try conclusions with its environment, the already existing sense of insecurity is reinforced by another motive; the child becomes conscious of its littleness, its helplessness, and its dependence upon adults.

For every child "to be grown up is a goal most passionately desired" (Dr. Wexberg). Even the healthy child feels the distance between himself and the 'grown-ups'; indeed, the sense of unequal ability, of inadequacy, furnishes the first impetus toward all development; it is the motive power that drives the human being onwards. But the goal of adult life looms before him only as a compass-bearing; he grows up, innocently, actively, and as a matter of course, into the community and its tasks, feeling confident of being able to do something useful.

The organically weak or ailing child has often already lost his innocence, his reasonableness, and his self-confidence. He cannot be active, for he is concerned with other things; he must observe, compare, try conclusions with his environment, and measure himself against other children who are more advanced and more capable. And he comes to the conclusion that he cannot keep up with the others, that he is left behind, that he is less capable and of less value than the others. Here we see the origin of what Adler calls the 'sense of inferiority,' which can be oppressive and burdensome, and indeed often unbearable, so that it is impossible to remain in this state of subjection, and the child must of necessity endeavour to rise above it. And now the law of compensation comes into operation, which Adler has found to be valid for the psychic life as well as for the physical.

The greater the sense of insecurity, the greater the drive towards reassurance; the more irksome the sense of inferiority, which may become an inferiority complex (by which Adler means the persistent appearance of the consequences of the sense of inferiority), the more intense is the striving for respect, recognition, consideration, and power! The minus must be turned into a plus; the deficiency must be replaced by superfluity.

Such a child can no longer undertake any useful activities; indeed he no longer has any confidence in his ability to do anything useful. 'Growing up' no longer looms before him as a goal, as a lode-star, pointing the way to follow; the tendency which now rules him no longer permits of an elastic adaptation to nullity. The child with the enhanced sense of inferiority, and the correspondingly intensified striving to become important, "is relying on a fixed point which does not really exist, and is entangled in the meshes of his fiction " (Adler).

This kind of fiction is defined in Hans Vaihinger's *Philosophie des Als-Ob* (" The Philosophy of As-Though ") as an auxiliary concept, an aid to thought, a useful assumption which facilitates the acquisition of knowledge. Just as the globe is divided into sections by meridians which have no real existence, but which can be utilized in navigation, so there are psychic fictions which one needs in order to find one's way amidst the chaos of life. People think in fictions, and make arrangements regarding the future, although it is quite uncertain whether they will be in existence when that future arrives; they assume that they will be, although they know very well that their assumption is a fiction, because otherwise they would be unable to cope with life.

The child with the enhanced sense of inferiority puts the fiction in the place of the reality, and does so *as though* he could reach his goal. This goal always looms before the child in some concrete form; he would like to be as tall, as strong, as superior, in short as powerful as his father or any other adult who appears to him especially pre-eminent. And now he spins his threads of phantasy toward this exalted point, as though he could reach his goal, which is actually unattainable. All the child's energies will be expended in serving this end; he must have respect, esteem, recognition. Since these do not appear to be attainable in any other way, he turns to modes of behaviour which will compel the grown-ups to give him close attention; constant complaints and disturbances, obstinacy, rage, outbursts of anger, lying, stealing (all active traits); or inability to concentrate, alleged inability to learn, forgetfulness, excessive sensitiveness, anxiety, timidity, shyness, solitariness (passive traits). Very often one finds active and passive traits commingled; that is, the child alters his mode of behaviour in accordance with the situation.

If he now finds himself in a situation which seems to him especially menacing, in which he (unconsciously) believes that he will not be able to escape from it by the methods hitherto employed, he resorts to intensified means. If, for example, on the birth of a brother or sister, the child finds that he is not, as heretofore, the centre of interest, or in the event of a sudden death, or when the family moves to another neighbourhood—in short, in all situations which involve unwelcome changes—in children of this type symptoms may make their appearance which are quite understandable if examined from the standpoint of individual-psychology.

Bed-wetting in a child who has previously been clean; difficulties in respect of food (eating so slowly that he has to spend hours over meals; eating only if someone will tell stories; lingering over mouthfuls of food without swallowing them, carried to the point of actual refusal to eat); gastric and intestinal disorders without organic changes; nocturnal shrieks of terror. Of course, to begin with, in the case of organic symptoms, the doctor should be consulted. But if no organic trouble can be detected, if the condition should be described as 'merely nervous,' then the case may properly be handled on the lines of Adler's teaching. In a case of bed-wetting a sensitive urinary system may offer a temptation to choose this particular symptom, and in the case of gastric and intestinal disorders, a sensitive digestive canal, etc. If one wishes to regard these symptoms correctly, it must be realized that the child, in situations which are prejudicial to his status, makes increased efforts to draw attention to himself. He enlists the defective or sensitive organ to serve his purpose, and by so doing compels those about him to give him closer attention, converting his weakness into strength. But in this case the psychic process is *unconscious*; a dynamism working upwards from below.

And here it should be noted that this unconscious dynamism, this device of enlisting a defective organ to serve a purpose, is to be seen, not only in children, but very often in adults also. It occurs in all cases of so-called 'organ neurosis.' The term 'neurosis' (derived from the Greek) really means a derangement of or injury to a nerve, but in psychiatry and in general parlance it is used to describe a persistent disturbance of the psychic equilibrium, which may manifest itself in organic symptoms, psychical phenomena, and defects of character. In all those cases in which organ neuroses are established there is no demonstrable anatomical alteration of the organ in question, but a functional disturbance due to a persistent psychic irritation.

According to Adler, the individual law of movement of a human being is developed in earliest childhood. Practical experience has shown that all the symptoms observable in difficult, psychopathic and ailing adults, are perceptible at a very early age in children, though often in quite different forms, so that the individual-psychologist pays very special attention to the development of the young child.

CHAPTER II

THE fact that the great majority of difficult and backward children, and also of difficult and psychopathic adults, belong to the type of the 'spoilt child,' the 'mollycoddle,' shows how much damage may be inflicted by an over-indulgent method of education; if only because the child is deceived, inasmuch as life, and the world, was represented to him in a shape which does not correspond with the reality. The young, inexperienced mother believes that she is being especially kind if she gives the child more help than is absolutely necessary when it first attempts to stand upright; if she supports it during its first attempts to walk, although such support is no longer necessary; if she imitates its first attempts to speak, and converses with it only in 'baby language'; and if, when it tries to grasp an object, she puts the latter into its hand. Not only the mother, however, but the father also, and other members of the family, all vie in saving the child exertion, often enough because they are too nervously irritable, or too indulgent, or too impatient to await the natural process of evolution, or—even more frequently—because they are afraid the child may injure itself. And in this way it may very well happen that its courage and activity are checked in their development.

If a child is permanently influenced in this way it grows up in the opinion that the people round about it are there simply to help it in all difficulties; so that it will become accustomed to expecting them to serve it. It will no longer rely on itself; it will always look to someone for help.

Such children, moreover, are in most cases absurdly spoilt, and—if circumstances permit of it—are overwhelmed with presents. So, inevitably, they form the opinion that the whole world exists for them alone, that without any effort on their part everything ought to fall into their laps. Every word, every least remark, is given a special significance; in the case of any organic insufficiency the child realizes that its mother is worrying about its physical condition; if it sees that the eating and digesting of its meals are the most important affairs in the world it naturally comes to believe that it must be a prince or princess. And here it must be noted that the phenomenon of the 'spoilt child' is to be encountered not only in a well-to-do environment, but, with corresponding modifications, in all social circles.

One day—unwarned and unprepared—such a child is confronted with the stark reality; generally when it first goes to its kindergarten or school; at all events, when it first ventures beyond the narrow limits of the family circle. Now it has to hold its own, on equal terms, among other children. Where is the mother on whom it has been accustomed to lean—where the support which it has hitherto enjoyed all its life? For the first time the child has to cope with something new, with strange children, with unfamiliar things.

But it is not accustomed to doing anything by itself; to acting independently; for the members of its family, who love it so dearly, have prevented it from exercising its independence. Its lack of self-confidence was not remedied by giving it opportunities of testing its independence; if possible it was actually intensified. The whole over-indulgent atmosphere of its home has helped to hinder the free development of the child's latent energies. And now, for the first time, it has to rely on itself.

Some, on this first day of school, cling anxiously to their mother, and seek, by their loud weeping, to prevent her from going away and leaving them: only by prolonged and kindly persuasion can they be quieted and induced to take their place among the other children. They may then make an anxious attempt to do so, but this—because of its uneasiness—may very well be a fiasco.

An experience of this kind—which, of course, would be repeated—was bound to discourage such a child, until in the end it would no longer venture further experiments, refusing to make any sort of effort. It is only too easy to realize that the child would be extremely unhappy in its school or kindergarten, and in any case would endeavour to escape from it; consciously, by means of open protest, and unconsciously making use of a defective organ, and suffering, perhaps, from attacks of nausea and vomiting before the mother leaves it.

Another variant: the child quietly allows its mother to take her departure, but then immediately makes itself unpleasantly conspicuous by aggressive and quarrelsome behaviour, refusing all co-operation unless it can be the leader, who seeks to depreciate others in order to seem important.

There are many variants that reveal the child's endeavours to enforce attention in some active manner, even though such activity may not be positively applied.

A much more difficult type is that of the spoilt or 'molly-coddle' child.

On its first day at school, when its mother is about to leave it, the child is in deadly terror. "They are going to leave me alone!" This terror, however, does not lead to an attempt to delay the mother's departure; the child's active rebellion is so effectively repressed that it can only quietly surrender. It looks on the ground if the other children speak to it; it does not reply to questions; it is shy and holds itself aloof. It hears the others talking and laughing, and longs to join them, but it cannot—it has too little self-confidence. It is sensible of the great distance between itself and other children, and suddenly realizes that it is not really a prince or princess at all, but less capable than the others, and inferior to them. This sudden fall from the skies inevitably sets the compensation-motive in operation. The child cannot bear to feel that it is less than the others; it wants to be regarded as their equal—or rather, it wants to be superior to the others. The greater the distance between desire and ability, the stronger the urge to be better than the others—cleverer, more powerful, superior. But how is this possible if the child is shy and 'stand-offish'?

Any one who has had occasion to observe a reclusive child in class will have to admit that no other child claims so much of the teacher's attention. The teacher is constantly making efforts to 'draw him out,' to get some response from him. He will try every means: friendliness, patience, affection, kindness, and finally—but then he is defeated—severity. The reclusive child is stronger; the victory is his! The more pains the teacher takes, the more stubbornly will the child exploit the means at his disposal. Of course, he knows nothing of these matters; but he has no confidence in himself, in his ability to compete with the others, and he therefore refuses to do so, since there is nothing that a spoilt child (or an adult who was once a spoilt child) fears so much as a defeat. So he takes refuge in his isolation, and celebrates his victories in his own fashion. The whole class regards him as a special case; the children talk about him and discuss him privately; so that he has achieved a sort of importance, though of a negative and useless kind.[1]

For that matter, a spoilt child intent on achieving his goal may give the impression of complete self-reliance, until he encounters some difficulty that reveals his impatience, irritability and helplessness. The decisive characteristics of such children are that they cannot endure the least anxiety; they never give, but always take; they always want everything for themselves, and endeavour in every way to draw tribute from those about them.

Adler stresses the fact that these difficult children are highly intelligent; they employ the means at their disposal for the attainment of their goal—the goal of superiority—in the most intelligent manner. Their actions are not merely reasonable, if by 'reasonable' we mean profitable in practical life.

Once more, then: The psychic life strives to overcome obstacles, to achieve completion, to change the minus sign for the plus. The so-called normal, healthy human being tries to adapt himself actively to life, and to reach the plus

[1] See "The Silent Child" in the "Practical Section."

value by some real achievement. The other type, who has no confidence in his power of achievement, makes the mistake of trying to gain the upper hand by personal superiority.

And so a spoilt child, such as we have described, unless a timely and expert education supervenes, may become an unhappy man, unsufferable to those about him, an enemy of society, or merely an isolated human being, who leads a lonely and embittered existence, which may end in melancholia, or even in suicide.

The child who is subjected to a regime of unloving severity is treated very differently from the spoilt child, yet this different treatment may in the end have very much the same results. Conceived, perhaps unwillingly, by a mother who feels no affection for him, he knows nothing of the care and watchfulness which are necessary for his normal development. Just as a flower needs sunlight in order to unfold, so a child needs love, and above all an atmosphere of kindly warmth (but not over-indulgent and relaxing). A loveless education does not provide such an atmosphere.

While the over-indulgent mother deprives the child of all stimulus to effort, the unloving governess or pedagogue—and very often a child's education may be unloving because it has lost its mother—leaves the child to cope with far too many difficulties. A very young child is confronted with tasks which it is still too undeveloped to perform; it attempts them, but its attempts are bound to fail, as it is still too undeveloped physically to perform them properly. In the event of repeated failure, followed perhaps by harsh expostulation, the child may come to believe that it is incapable of anything. Such a notion, once conceived, will of course inhibit any further development. Here is a vicious circle: Something goes wrong, and one no longer has confidence in oneself; and because one no longer has confidence in oneself, and tackles everything in a spirit of self-distrust, the possibility of any further success is excluded beforehand. The unloving guardian or teacher denies that the child is capable of doing anything, and so, of course, it cannot do anything properly. Such comments as: " You'll never come to anything in life! " or " You'll never make a good job of anything! " etc. may help to confirm the child in this opinion.

At the same time, it knows that it wishes to accomplish something, that it does take pains, and it is conscious of the incessant blame and nagging as a monstrous injustice, a frightful incubus, against which it secretly rebels.

If such a mode of education is reinforced by punishment, and perhaps even by blows, the protest and secret rebellion of the child may become so intense that any useful activity on the child's part is out of the question.

Even in these cases the child proceeds intelligently in applying the means at its disposal, accommodating its mode of behaviour to the situation. Such children will usually do badly in school, thereby punishing ambitious parents by striking at their most sensitive point.

The so-called ' stupid ' child is very often the product of a loveless education, in which no effort has been made to become intimately acquainted with the child. Perhaps, on asking questions after its first lack of success, it may have received such replies as, " A fool can ask more questions than ten wise men can answer," etc., so that it gets out of the habit of asking questions; it deliberately seems stupid, no longer takes an interest in anything, and its range of activities is contracted; which is just what it is counting upon, for no one can expect or demand anything of a stupid child.

Such children may exhibit the greatest variety in their modes of behaviour, which are readily understood if examined from the standpoint of individual-psychology.

At home, in the presence of the unloving adult, they will perhaps play the part of the well-behaved child, while they seek compensation by tormenting and tyrannizing over their younger brothers and sisters. At school they may be hostile and refractory, or they may behave like simpletons, making grimaces, laughing and playing silly tricks, and giving trouble in every way. What are we to make of this, or of all the different modes of behaviour, in different environments, of the same child, who often gives one the impression of being ' two different children '?

As a matter of fact, such a child is merely employing different means to achieve the same end. The child who has been discouraged by unloving (or by over-indulgent) treatment at home no longer has any confidence in his powers of real achievement, and turns to the methods at his disposal in order to enforce attention. Again, he is intelligent, but not reasonable!

Such children may also manifest other modes of behaviour: so-called childish aberrations and sexual viciousness.

The retention of childish aberrations—thumb-sucking, nail-biting, grimacing, nose-picking, infantile stuttering—is always found in children who have lost confidence in themselves. If they think themselves threatened, or feel unequal to the situation confronting them, they make use of this means of compensation in order to restore their diminished self-confidence. Thumb-sucking is a survival from infancy; it is a substitute for the pleasurable function of sucking the breast; at the same time the child derives satisfaction from its occupation with its own body. The very fact that it needs such satisfaction, and cannot derive satisfaction from an activity befitting its age, is evidence of discouragement.

The same may be said of the rest of the above-named symptoms, by which the child's protest is expressed, and which naturally provoke constant admonitions and prohibitions from adult observers. However, it succeeds in drawing constant attention to itself.

Stammering, again, is an expression of a sense of inadequacy; of weakness and inferiority, of subjection, and is a particularly useful expedient, since it appeals both to the patience and to the compassion of the person against whom it is applied. It may also serve to justify an abstention. Even in adults stammering serves to justify abstention or abdication; offering a legitimate excuse for refusing to cope with the ordinary tasks of life. Stammering—whether in a child or in an adult—always betrays a hesitating attitude toward the tasks of life—the 'yes—but . . .' of the neurotic.

Of sexual aberrations, the most frequent is masturbation, which, however, is to be regarded merely as a symptom of the child's general deportment. Originally—in the very young child—masturbation is usually provoked by an organic irritation, and, like thumb-sucking, constitutes an occupation with the child's own body which affords him gratification. It has nothing to do with sexuality, even if it is persisted in when the child is a little older; here again it is to be regarded as a means of self-expression on the part of an intimidated, dejected little creature. In one way masturbation may be extremely dangerous to the child. Parents and pedagogues often regard this habit with horror, because they attribute to it the most complicated sexual consequences. The child convicted of the practice will very often perceive, through the reproaches, admonitions and threats of his teacher, that in this he has a means which can be employed to great effect in his conflict with the 'grown-ups.' Adler, as the first principle of education, insists that one must never become involved in a conflict with the child; for the child is the stronger, and will be victorious. He even considers that in our present stage of culture the greatest power is wielded by the infant. The child, who has withdrawn from the true theatre of war—real, active life—is victorious on the secondary field of battle if he can persuade the adult to follow him thither. So, in the case of masturbation, despite severity and punishment, the discouraged child will persist in the habit. Threats of such consequences as imbecility, incurable illness, death, etc. should in any case be avoided, for they may have disastrous consequences. Attempts to break the habit will be all the more unsuccessful in proportion as the child is more discouraged; they will evoke feelings of guilt which will give the habit a compulsive force.

If the practice is retained beyond the age of puberty, until the time when a man ought to find his way to persons of the other sex, it must be regarded as the mark of an isolated character, who evades the solution of the sexual problem, just as he evades the solution of all the rest of life's problems. Even here the symptom is characteristic of the general attitude of the personality.

The individual-psychological method, whether applied to the child or the adult, never proceeds to the treatment of symptoms, but aims at the readjustment of the whole personality. If it succeeds in effecting such readjustment the symptoms disappear.

It follows, then, that both an over-indulgent and a loveless education or an unduly severe education—which need not be actually unloving, but which by constant nagging and scolding deprives the child of all *joie de vivre* and buoyancy—may lead to the same consequences: they divert the child from the straight path of real performance, which leads to achievements of obvious value, into devious ways and spurious satisfactions. Both methods have the same result: they hamper the activity and sap the spirit of the child and make it a bad co-operator.

CHAPTER III

By the *family constellation* we understand:

1. The mutual relation of the parents and its effect on the child.
2. The position of the child in the sequence of brothers and sisters.

If we look back on the events of the last thirty years we shall realize the difficulties that beset the present epoch: the first world war, with all its consequences (not only in the combatant countries); sickness and adversity, impoverishment and hopelessness, then revolution, inflation, and economic crises; the seizure of power by despotic governments, which involved repression and persecution, for reasons of political conviction, religious belief, or race, for large sections of the populations; and finally a new world war, exceeding in its enormity anything that the most morbid imagination could have conceived. When we consider the effect of all these events upon everyday life—how these afflictions have cast their shadows over so many families, and in particular how they have affected relations between men and women—we cannot wonder that in many marriages, which were formerly characterized by harmony and agreement, tensions and conflicts have made their appearance which could not fail to affect the child.

The atmosphere of the parental home, the vital atmosphere which surrounds the young child, is inevitably an essential factor of his development.

Whether a child obtains his first experiences of life as a member of a harmonious family circle—whether he witnesses helpfulness, neighbourliness and, above all, respect for others, or whether he grows up, as it were, in a hostile country, where he is forced to observe indifference, hatred, and detraction of others, is a matter of great importance.

Even in cases where the parents make the sincerest efforts to conceal their differences from the child, the constant tension of the atmosphere may exert an unfavourable influence. But if he is an actual witness of serious conflicts between his father and mother—the two persons who for him are the embodiment of security—he experiences a shock, a loss of confidence, which may have its consequences much later in life. Something will be revealed to the child, a fragment of life will be exhibited, which it cannot yet understand, and by which it must therefore be greatly startled.

Distrust of other human beings, inability to make contact with them, and a later aversion from marriage may be referred back to such childish experiences. In such situations it often happens that the child is the bone of contention—that he stands between the conflicting parties, and is a victim of their mutual aggression; and it may then happen that he secretly takes the side of one of his parents, and that this partiality results in a feeling of guilt, so that his mind is not at rest. But this, of course, does not mean that he will never exploit the situation to his own benefit.

Of the greatest importance in respect of his development is the child's position in the sequence of his brothers and sisters. To the only child, as a general thing, all that we have said concerning an over-indulgent education may be applied. In many cases the only child has to suffer from the defects of an education which is well intended, but is bound to be defective, as the parent's or teacher's attitude toward the child is incorrect. For the only child, who grows up regarding himself in the light of a little prince or princess, the *mot d'ordre* which is characteristic of every difficult child and every adult neuropath is especially valid: "All or nothing! I must and will have all that I can get people to give me—or nothing; rather than exert myself, I will go without it!"

The development of the child is bound to assume an especially catastrophic form if parents who have done their utmost to make their child incapable of effort by their over-indulgence thereafter make exaggerated claims upon him. Most parents of an only child wish to see in him the realization of all the hopes whose fulfilment has been withheld from them. Experiments are made on the child; even before he goes to school he must be a little scholar. They try to make him understand ideas which he is as yet too undeveloped to grasp. And then they grow impatient; often making such observations as: "You just wait until you go to school!" or, "You'll never learn anything!" and so on. We have already noted how dangerous such remarks may be, even when they are not intended seriously; and once more it must be stressed that a child who is already discouraged may easily discover that he really cannot learn anything. Such are the apparently incapable and unintelligent children who are complete failures at school or in the kindergarten.

The eldest child is always for a time the only child, and is therefore exposed to the same dangers as the only child. But even when the situation is altered by the birth of a second child, the eldest encounters great difficulties of another kind. An only child is generally prepared for the birth of a brother or sister; he is told, for example, that very soon he will have a little brother or sister . . . and how lovely it will be for him to have someone to play with! (Only children, one must remember, are always lonely.) And now, suddenly, the other child is there, and the only child that was perceives that it is not at all lovely, that he has been deceived, and that he has lost his former, central position. He feels neglected; he feels that he has been dethroned. In most cases he then protests against the supposed treachery of his mother in the greatest variety of ways (and very often even with bodily symptoms); forms of protest which are regarded by the adults as naughtiness, and which are followed, for the child, by unpleasant consequences and punishments.

This seems to him an additional proof that the love which has hitherto been lavished upon him is withdrawn, and that he is being ill-treated. This tragedy of dethronement is experienced not only by the eldest child, but also by the child who is the youngest until a successor appears.

A further difficulty may arise in this way: his responsible

position as the eldest child may be impressed upon the child as something so onerous (especially if his parents are dead) that he may become discouraged. Or the child's ambition may be so stimulated that the actual purpose of his activities recedes into the background, and the child aims only at a factitious prestige, an apparent success. Suffering from a very authoritarian education, the eldest child often tries to help himself by passing the burden on to his younger brothers and sisters, ordering them about or tormenting them. He thus finds a way of displaying his striving for power.

Adler has found that the eldest child often displays a conservative trait in his general attitude, and a respect for traditional authority; while in the second child he often observed revolutionary tendencies. Following up this discovery, he studied the biographies of eminent men—thinkers, authors, and artists—and found his observations confirmed. He explained the matter thus: the second child, especially if he is not *much* younger than his senior, has always before his eyes someone with whom he is trying to catch up—someone who in years, and usually in stature and influence, holds a superior position in the family. If there is a third child—who, as the youngest, will usually be spoilt—the second child will have to make still greater efforts in order to assert himself; he will then, so to speak, have to conduct operations on two fronts simultaneously.

At the same time, the second child of three may adopt a totally different attitude. Precisely because he fills the middle position his behaviour may show an increasing divergence from that of his senior and his junior; it may be intimidated, or impeccable, or by compliant amiability he may seek to assure himself of a place in the sun. One can never assume anything beforehand; one must always determine the fact by exact observation, because " it can be just the other way about."

In large families groups may be formed, in which the same phenomena may often be observed.

The youngest child, we know, has often a privileged position; nevertheless, this position is threatened from many directions. On the one hand, as the 'baby,' he is subject to the difficulties of the spoilt or cossetted child; while his privileged position is often envied by his older brothers and sisters. On the other hand, the youngest child, especially if the difference between him and the others is not very great, may easily find himself driven into a very burdensome rivalry. He will do his utmost to achieve, as far as possible, all that his older brothers and sisters can do, and this may lead to an excessive strain upon his faculties, or to an attempt to achieve a spurious success. In this curious juxtaposition of cossetting on the one hand, and repression on the other, the youngest child often contrives to hold his own by endeavouring to cling as long as possible to the safe position of the youngest child, deliberately remaining 'the baby' longer than is really necessary—that is, if his mother's attitude favours this course. Such children rarely or never become independent and self-confident.

Yet the pressure exerted by older brothers and sisters may develop a very different attitude in the youngest child. It may evoke a tremendous effort, acting as a powerful stimulus, which will lead to great achievements. Pioneers and leaders in all departments of life have often been the youngest children of their families, and even in sagas and fairy-tales the heroic role is often allotted to the youngest son.

It often looks as though the various children of a family are stimulating and encouraging one another. For example, the eldest child, possibly influenced by the atmosphere of his home, is interested in intellectual matters, and being thus unconsciously stimulated, he may go far in this direction. The second child, instinctively feeling that in this respect he cannot equal the eldest, unconsciously chooses some other field in which to distinguish himself; he may, for example, exhibit great manual skill and dexterity. One child has a gift for languages; another is hopeless as a linguist, but is exceptionally good at arithmetic, etc. Where there are many brothers and sisters, of course, this kind of influence may run through the family, and all sorts of variants may be observed. Individual-psychology has characterized this phenomenon as unconscious training in various directions.

After what has just been said the reader might feel that there cannot be such a thing as a normal child, since, after all, every child is either an only child, or the eldest child, or the youngest child, or occupies an intermediate position.

However, it has already been stated that the factors which Adler has distinguished do not *necessarily* exert an unfavourable influence. On the other hand, he has often observed that the position of the child in the family may produce unfortunate results. In dealing with adult patients one is constantly confronted with the profound repercussions of aggression in early childhood. If a child feels that he is being ill-treated, and that a brother or sister is preferred before him, this attitude persists in the adult, whether or not the feeling was really justified. It is never the objective facts that matter, but only the opinions which the individual has formed of the objective facts. The unconscious conflict between brothers and sisters plays an enormous part in the development of the child. Two tendencies are always present: the tendency to feel that one is oppressed, and to protest against this oppression; which leads to the second tendency: the longing to dominate others.

One point must now be mentioned which has not hitherto been considered: the part played by the sex of the child.

Here we must keep the fact in mind that for some decades—actually since the close of the nineteenth century—the cultural relations between men and women have been undergoing a revolutionary change. The period of the first world war represented a phase of transition from a millenial masculine culture, tantamount to a suppression of the female sex, toward a movement of assimilation whose final aim was the complete equality of the sexes. In some fields this aim was already achieved; not, however, through a gradual organic process, the precondition of all healthy evolution, but through an enormously accelerated tempo, through revolutionary changes and fitful developments resulting from the war.

Although at the present time, at the bidding of stern necessity, the two sexes have in practice been confronted with equally exacting tasks—which, in most cases, they have successfully performed—yet it must not be forgotten that even the younger generation belongs, in point of origin, to the age of masculine culture, in which men were regarded as strong, powerful, and superior, and women as weak and inferior. In the not very remote past this conception held its own even in the nursery; for example, when a little girl, at the birth of a little brother, heard the people about her exclaim, "Thank God, it's a boy!" On every side she was confronted with this valuation; the privileged position of the male sex was for her a matter of experience; so that she was bound to acquire the belief that she—as a female—must be an inferior being. In addition to all other factors, the erroneous estimation of the role of sex helped—and often enough it still helps to-day—to produce in the girl a feeling of inferiority. And so a greater compensation is required; the girl has to make greater efforts to show that she is not merely 'just a girl,' but that she is just as good as, and, indeed, wants to show that she is even better than a boy.

After what has already been said, the fact that her efforts are not always of a useful nature need not be emphasized. Yet the great stress laid upon the woman's comparative weakness may have the result that the girl may turn her weakness into strength, exploiting her dependence and helplessness at the cost of others, especially if her family encourages her in such a course. And very great harm will be done to the girl if the inferior rôle is forced upon her.

But even the boy cannot congratulate himself on the results of this false valuation. He was conscious from his earliest childhood—to some extent he is still conscious to-day—of the higher valuation of his sex; so that he must try to be as masculine as possible—and this calls for increased effort. The seed of the tension between the sexes, the seed of conflict, of the struggle for power, was sown, and to some extent is still being sown, in the nursery.

Care should be taken that children who are already able to appreciate the distinction are not allowed to wear the clothes of the other sex; that is, boys should not be allowed to dress as girls, or girls as boys. Such a practice may easily lead to mental confusion; the child will not be quite clear in its mind as to the roles of the sexes. We find, in the treatment of perversions, homosexuality, etc., that from earliest childhood there has been a history of uncertainty, nourished by such practices, from which has arisen an aversion from the rôle of the patient's sex; manifesting itself by sexual deviations and retreat from the normal solution of the sexual problems.

CHAPTER IV

In the last two chapters we have spoken of the injurious effects of early rearing, which can be greatly diminished by enlightenment and instruction; at all events, one may hope that such mitigations will be increasingly possible.

But the social environment into which a child is born, or into which he is drawn in later life, is seen at the present time to be all but inaccessible to human and beneficent influence.

Unfavourable social conditions may very seriously inhibit the development of the human being. The mere fact that a child does not receive proper care and adequate nourishment means that his physical development is bound to suffer injury. Lack of care, of nourishing food, of light and air, favour maladies which will not receive adequate treatment; and organic deficiencies cannot receive the necessary attention. The mother is at work; the eldest of the family—herself a child—has to look after her younger brothers and sisters. Inevitably sins of omission are committed which may have grievous results. The child, as it grows up, learns to recognize social differences. Playing in the street and at school it sees that other children have better homes, are better dressed and better fed. It hears of toys, of films, and other delights which are inaccessible to the poor child, and it speaks of them at home. The parents, who are tired and worried, and often even unemployed, turn a deaf ear to such talk. They make bitter comments on the injustice of fate, which allots to one man a brilliant position in life, and to another nothing but toil and anxiety. In the case of children suffering from organic deficiencies, or discouraged by a depressing home, such remarks may fall upon fertile soil. Such children have no confidence that honest work will ever enable them to taste the pleasures that seem to them worth striving for. They see and hear so often that work will never get one anywhere, and the longing for a better life is so great that this becomes the goal for which they strive. Here again we see the urge to get to the top from underneath. They conceive a hatred for all who are better off than they; and they consider that they have a perfect right to take advantage of others and to annex little trifles that do not belong to them. The joy of possession is enhanced by the stimulating consciousness that they have done something forbidden, something prohibited by laws which are made by the people whom the child regards with hostility. When he has grown a little older, if his dishonest tricks have often been crowned with success, he becomes bolder and applies himself to larger affairs. He has lost all hope of ever being able to do anything useful, and must henceforth devote himself to futile undertakings. Sooner or later he is caught and brought up before the children's court, and is sent to a special school. Here he comes into contact with people who devote themselves to the most self-sacrificing efforts, in some cases with excellent results. But the most devoted efforts can do nothing to undo the injury which the child's character has suffered unless the necessary psychological basis is provided, as it is in many countries. For it must be realized that in institutions of this kind numbers of children are brought together, who, in consequence of years of unprofitable training, have accumulated such a store of hatred, that it is easy for them to bring the new-comer, who is already discouraged, over to their side. As a general thing, correctional education does not help to give those who find themselves on the shady side of life a new attitude to life. On the contrary, as a rule they are still further discouraged; they go still further to the bad; they continue to follow unprofitable courses, until at last they are convicted of crime. Punishment—as people are gradually coming to realize—does not tend to transform the offender's character. After serving his sentence he usually returns to society still more discouraged, and inspired by still greater hostility. For such men, unfortunately, it is generally very difficult to return to active life, and sometimes even impossible, although there are institutions which undertake the task of restoring the released prisoner to civic life. But whatever such institutions may do they are utterly inadequate, and the only possible result is that the great majority of ex-prisoners are driven to return to their criminal courses. Society is not as yet sufficiently conscious of the fact that every individual bears his share of the guilt of the others (" Every one is guilty towards all and of everything," in Dostoievski's words); that unfavourable social conditions, together with organic deficiencies and faulty education, may evoke and exacerbate feelings of inferiority. The inevitable result is compensation, which may have the force of an obsession. Owing to the delusion that they are not capable of achieving anything by honest means such men are often driven into crooked ways, and thus into vagabondage or crime.

Happily, however, the further development of those who come from an unfavourable social *milieu* is not bound to assume such an unfortunate form. The most valuable work in all departments of life has been done by men who came from such an environment. In all these cases it was apparent that the spur to successful compensation or over-compensation was provided by the severity of the struggle for a livelihood.

This survey cannot be conducted without reference to the vastly greater number of those who in respect of their birth and education, and the nature of their work, belonged to more favourable social circles, but who subsequently, out of political conviction, belief, or racial origin, were condemned to such circumstances as we have described, and often to very much harsher conditions.

Countless families have been torn apart; some of their members going overseas—mostly at a venture—in order to seek a new home and a new life; meeting, very often, with grievous disappointment; while those who remained behind, under an oppressive government, faced a life without prospects, and were finally deported as slave labourers. It is needless to enlarge on the disastrous effect which such experiences must have upon children.

But it is good to know that in spite of all this we can point to a number of cases of successful compensation and over-compensation, in which young people—and even the old—impelled by necessity, and by their responsibilities toward their families, and their fellow-creatures, have sought and found new ways of life. And further, that a great number of those whose lot was the hardest have accepted it with courage and dignity.

In the last three chapters of this book we have sought to describe a number of typical developmental processes which, in the event of the unsuccessful compensation of organic inferiority, under the influence of other unfavourable factors, are liable to different variations as regards the development of character. But it must be clearly understood that life cannot be reduced to types; that we are dealing merely with examples, and that every case must be considered individually.

Although the law of compensation holds good for all psychic life, and although the unprofitable activities of child or adult must be regarded as the form assumed by an unsuccessful compensation, we must never approach a case with a scheme in mind, with a preconceived opinion. Life expresses itself in an infinity of shades, nuances, and forms, and we must always begin by asking: what is the plan of life, the individual dynamic law, of this particular person?

Individual-psychology provides us with the instrument forged by Adler as the result of his medical practice: one must study the individual in his bearing, in his general mode of behaviour, in his attitude toward his fellow-creatures, in his manner of dealing with his vital problems; one must know his plans, his memories, his dreams, his fantasies. Once his purpose is known to us we can understand all the forms in which his life expresses itself, and only then shall we be in a position to intervene, to help and heal and reconstruct.

CHAPTER V

To summarize the findings of the foregoing survey: the emergence of intensified feelings of inferiority in the child may be referred to factors of two kinds: to biological factors (constitutional weakness and organic insufficiencies) and to sociological factors, which were distinguished as influences of education, the family, and the environment.

Adler began by giving the closest attention to the biological factors, to constitutional weakness, and above all to inherited, innate organic inferiority, inherited with life itself. These seemed to him to be of quite special significance.[1] Gradually, however, he came to emphasize no less strongly the sociological factors which can be summed up in the concept 'environment'; the environment which is to be understood as the totality of the circumstances into which a human being is born, that is, the family and the social *milieu.*

First and last, the organic inferiority of the child must be taken into account just like any other difficulty with which the individual has to cope; and the influences of his environment may help or hinder him in respect of his attitude toward it. How far they may do so is shown by the example mentioned in Chapter I: the case of Hermann Unthan, who was born without arms, and who, in spite of this defect, trained himself to become a useful member of society. His father, a village schoolmaster, laid down three fundamental principles when the child was born:

1. He must never be pitied or commiserated by those about him.
2. He must never be helped with or relieved of any task which he himself was capable of performing.
3. His feet must always be bare.

Thanks to these precautions he was able to develop and train

[1] *Studie über Minderwertigkeit von Organen* (Adler). Published Urban and Schwarzenberg, Vienna, Berlin, 1907.

his legs and feet to such purpose that he was able to study music, for which he had a great natural aptitude, and to play the violin, and at the age of seventeen he was able to give a concert in the Leipzig 'Gewandhaus.' The critics, on the whole, were highly appreciative, though in an interview the question was debated whether it would not be better if such a person were, for æsthetic reasons, to refrain from making a public appearance on the concert platform. Unthan accepted the hint without bitterness, and took active steps to find some other means of livelihood. He went on to the variety stage, on which he performed for more than forty years, appearing in all parts of the globe, and winning a name for himself. On the outbreak of the first world war he toured the hospitals, lectured to wounded soldiers who had lost arms or legs, and consoled the despairing, not only by his example, but by showing and teaching them how by exercise and training they could best make up for the loss of a limb. Later on Unthan became an instructor in a great home for cripples; in short, he was a man whose activities were definitely of a positive and useful character. It must be admitted that here was a cripple suffering from a grievous and innate physical defect, of a kind which is fortunately of rare occurrence. How was he able to develop his abilities in such a sane and healthy way?

Simply because, owing to his father's attitude, he did not see his defect as those about him saw it; because, in consequence of this defect, he had to make exceptional efforts; his first little successes encouraged him and helped him to do still better; so that by an unprecedented course of training he was able to teach other limbs to take the place of his missing arms.

This example proves very clearly the correctness of the psychological principle that the individual's development depends not on what he brings into the world with him, but rather on what he does with it, or how he uses it.[2] His own

[2] Adler describes his individual-psychology as a "psychology of use," in contrast to the "psychology of possession."

attitude toward his body and his organic deficiency is the important thing, and this attitude may be formed by, and may depend upon, the attitude of those around him, by whom the child is influenced. From the first days of his life he orientates himself upon his environment, and uses his experiences, his adventures, to form and establish his individual law of movement, and to build up his psychic structure with the co-operation of organic factors. But *how* all the experiences emanating from the body and the environment are elaborated, utilized, and evaluated by the child cannot be ascertained beforehand. They are merely *building-stones* of which the creative energy of the child disposes as it pleases, in order to find its way out of a situation with which it is unable to cope. This way, after a certain amount of practice, is adopted, with its specific characteristics, and reveals itself as a dynamic law which clings to the individual throughout his life, and determines his thoughts, his feelings, his desires and his actions. In this dynamic law the child's opinion of himself and his environment is expressed: his estimate of his own powers, and the powers of those with whom he has to deal, formed at a time when he cannot as yet express his adventures and experiences in words and concepts, but can only digest them emotionally. For this reason this opinion—and accordingly the dynamic law—will very often be erroneous and incomplete.

The most important task of the pedagogue, according to Adler, is not merely to ensure that favourable influences prevail, but to note very exactly what the creative powers of the child make of them, so that even in the case of a very young child erroneous opinions and mistaken attitudes can be recognized in time, and can be duly modified and corrected.

This principle of individual-psychology—that what is of crucial importance in the development of the individual is not what he brings into the world with him, but rather the use he makes of what he has brought—is a revolutionary conception, for it is tantamount to a declaration of war against the generalization of an established scientific theory, the theory of inherited capacities.

It is not surprising that Adler has been violently attacked on account of his ideas, for we have grown too accustomed to speaking of the inheritance of qualities and defects, especially in cases where medical and pedagogic efforts have been ineffectual. It is very natural in such cases to speak of inheritance, but it is not very useful or practical. Such pessimism condemns all our efforts to futility. If we really believe that in such cases an inevitable destiny must prevail we may as well fold our hands and leave everything to fate. Of course, there are cases in which an inherited taint cannot be questioned, and Adler—the physician—knew very well that the poisoning of the organism by certain infections, or by alcohol, may have disastrous effects on the offspring; that constitutional weaknesses and organic defects, and tendencies thereto, can be inherited. He knew also that the individual is born with a vast number of vestiges, tendencies, and possibilities of a psychic and spiritual character. But it is impossible to say *which* of these vestiges, tendencies and possibilities are suppressed and disappear, and which, owing to compensation or over-compensation, make their appearance in quite different forms. However, we can tell what is not inherited, but acquired; what has been developed in conflict with the outer world, and in contact with the social *milieu*.

Moreover, individual-psychology refers many characters which have commonly been regarded as inherited to other factors; so that we need not give way to the paralysis or the pessimism that looks for the emergence of inherited defects.

Generally speaking, people are greatly averse to surrendering the theory of inherited faculties—and especially that part of the theory which refers to innate talents or innate lack of certain talents. Here again Adler has made war upon preconceived opinions, and it will be readily understood that this has excited much opposition, for after all, every one flatters himself by the delusion that he possesses natural gifts. The notion of natural gifts is used, by those who lay claim to them, to enhance their own sense of personality, while the apparently ungifted person accepts the odium of incapacity in order to shield and protect himself, and as an excuse for the fact that he makes no efforts. At the same time, natural incapacity is the best justification of the pedagogue who cannot show any results.

The very fact that the poet's dictum, " Against stupidity even the gods fight in vain " has attained the status of a proverb, tells us to what an extent this notion fills a general want. If the delusion of natural capacity had not taken such a hold upon every one we must have learned, long ago, by practical experience, even without Adler, that it is a delusion. For example: how can we explain the fact that a child who is regarded as absolutely incapable in respect of a particular subject, will suddenly begin to work at it, gradually improving, and finally doing very well, if he comes under a new teacher, who understands how to arouse his interest and conjure up a positive attitude toward the subject?

Just as frequently the reverse of this process may be observed; a child who is regarded as having a talent for a particular subject is so unfavourably affected by a change of teacher that he begins to retrogress and finally shows himself to be incapable of doing anything.

From his own experience Adler learned the truth about inherited capacity. In the lowest class at school he was such a bad scholar that he was regarded as mentally deficient, and his father was advised to take him away from school and have him taught a handicraft. His father did not take this advice, but made the boy continue his studies. In mathematics he was an absolute failure until one day, when he was in the lowest class but one, he suddenly perceived the solution of a problem which had baffled the whole class.

This experience encouraged him, so that he took an interest in mathematics from that day onwards, and became the best mathematician in the class.

Adler has coined the maxim: " Anyone can do anything! "—a statement which will not find ready acceptance. But one must understand what is meant by it. It means that everybody, unless he is a pathological subject, is born with unsuspected possibilities, which, if they are developed and fostered—above all, provided they are not suppressed and disregarded—may reveal faculties capable of great achievements. How can we tell when we meet someone—even a very young child—how much discouragement and frustration he has experienced in his life hitherto? Only if one had an abundance of human material at one's disposal, which one could observe from the moment of birth, while protecting it from all disturbing influences, one could perhaps, after many years, say something more definite on this point; but such inquiries are of course impossible. For which very reason the pedagogue should go about his work on the optimistic principle: " Anyone can do anything! "

Here, perhaps, we should once again remind the reader that Adler, through his experience as a practising neurologist, was able to obtain a profound insight into the psychic life of human beings, and to ascertain the laws which operated therein; the urge toward self-command and improvement, the movement upwards from below, from the minus to the plus situation.

But if he had contented himself with the statement of his discoveries his achievements would not have possessed their acknowledged significance in the fields of psychotherapy and pedagogy. Adler, as the result of his observations, was led into suggesting entirely new pedagogical methods, and in so doing he devised a prophylaxis of nervous affections and deformations of character.

This description would be incomplete if no mention were made of certain important pedagogical principles for which we have to thank individual-psychology.

We have already spoken of the optimistic principle at the root of the Adlerian maxim: " Anyone can do anything! " A child's education must be optimistic. By ' optimism ' we do not mean the unthinking attitude of a man who believes that he has a right to specially favoured treatment from life, or fate, or Providence, or whatever one calls the supreme power, and who always expects everything to happen as he desires, without any particular effort on his part.

Optimism here means the confident attitude of a man who devotes himself to serious effort, and who, being conscious that he has done the utmost of which he is capable, feels confident that he may await a favourable result. The pedagogue—and not only the professional schoolmaster, but everyone who is occupied in guiding and forming human beings—must be an optimist: that is, he must be completely and profoundly convinced that unsuspected possibilities are dormant in every human being, and it is his vocation to help to bring them to light. He must have patience; he must know how to wait; that is, he must not be hasty and ambitious, he must not strive for power and prestige, but must always be ready to step back and make way for another. Why is it so excessively difficult to fulfil these requirements? Because most of us, in our own lack of assurance, feel ourselves personally assailed if we do not succeed, if things do not happen as we wish; for example, if a child does not behave as we wish, we feel to blame and unsure of our authority. This feeling that we have suffered a defeat, that we have been degraded, compels us to seek for compensation, for consideration, even the show of consideration. We have spoken repeatedly, in the foregoing chapters, of the danger of this false striving for consideration; and we have seen how easily it may become a struggle for power. For this reason the individual-psychologist tells us, plainly and urgently: The teacher must be taught!

Such demands have always been made. If one studies the history of pedagogy one is constantly finding, in all the systems of the more eminent teachers, in the writings of thinkers and philosophers, individual elements of Adler's doctrine, although the philosophical background may be entirely different from his. For Adler, his discoveries constitute a philosophy, a science of human nature. They demand the unconditional cancellation of the struggle for personal power, and therefore the education of the educator.

Anyone who will seriously undertake the task of educating himself, who is prepared to examine and control himself, will obtain, through the experience acquired in the practice of individual-psychology, the equipment for a truer approach to life, which is possible only to those who have gone through "an inner ripening process" (Dr. Fritz Künkel). And in particular, anyone who has anything to do with education should proceed to an examination of his own attitude whenever he is confronted with a refusal or denial. The technique of individual-psychology will reveal connexions which were formerly invisible. He will find in himself the trend which Adler detected—the urge from below upwards—which every individual can discover in himself, in varying degrees of intensity. Under Adler's guidance he will realize that the dynamic law formed in earliest childhood is not necessarily more decisive because it tends to inhibit development. He will gradually come to understand that everyone is capable—quite independently of his physical qualities and his environment—of correcting attitudes and modes of behaviour which have proved to be defective on the basis of his *insight*—that is, he is capable of deciding to alter his attitude.

Human beings can never be perfect; they are liable to error and to failure; but they should constantly endeavour to progress "from greater errors to lesser" (Adler).

The educationist who has made this discovery must draw the necessary consequences. In his new attitude he will realize that it is especially dangerous to make a complete surrender of the false, rigid authority on which he has generally relied. This happened after the first world war, when it underwent transformation into exaggerated aberrations in the opposite direction, which caused, to some extent, the restoration of this false authority as the guiding principle of pedagogy.

In the foregoing chapters it has been repeatedly pointed out that oppressive authority provokes protest and defiance. The refractory child adapts his behaviour to that of his teacher; doing precisely the contrary of what his teacher desires. Such children—and such adults—live in an attitude of protest, in constant expectation of threat or oppression, and always ready for conflict. But even when the child's rebelliousness appears to have been broken by a strict, authoritative education, even when he apparently complies with authority, this does not as yet signify a forward step, but only a compromise, an adaptation to a given situation, the result of considering what he had better do. The child's self-confidence is not thereby increased.

Spurious authority means oppression and compulsion, lifeless obedience, timid subordination, bowing to superior force; but it can never evoke a voluntary, cheerful co-operation. Moreover, this kind of authority has yet another dangerous aspect; when children are kept down by authority they are liable to seek what advantages may be derived from the situation; they take refuge under authority, and allow it to determine their actions, renouncing all personal responsibility. Such individuals can never have confidence in themselves, for they have not developed self-confidence by independent action. They will always be timid and distrustful, dreading any responsibility, and evading the problems of life.

The reproach has been brought against individual-psychology that it undermines the most important pedagogical principle—authority—and that to some extent it opens the door to chaos and madness. This is an error, a total misconception of Adler's doctrine. This absolutely requires an authority: the authority of the idea, or the fact; which in this case amounts to the same thing. It is merely the spurious authority, unsupported by reason, insisting only on personal acknowledgment, that individual-psychology seeks to discard; because this kind of authority brings other evils in its train.

The authoritative type cannot dispense with esteem. He emphasizes, by his authoritative gestures, the difference between himself and other men; he offers himself as the model of perfection, which others are to take as a standard. Even in the schools the system of appraisement, as seen in the publication of results and the issue of certificates, is taken very seriously. Of course, it is impossible to avoid some estimation of the child's performance, for the child himself is bound to know when and how far he fails to do what is required of him. But such estimation—especially if it is negative in character—must never so discourage the child that in his dread of further failure he no longer dares to attempt success. In so far as it is necessary to allude to his inadequacy, he must if possible be shown that there are other subjects in which he could do well, and, above all, it must be made clear to him that others had to put forth their utmost effort in order to succeed. One should encourage him, even when he finds the work difficult, to keep up with the others, to practise, and to discipline himself, and explain that it is only by such means that he can achieve greater self-confidence and therefore do better work.

After what has already been said it is almost superfluous to speak of punishment, for it has been proved that punishment can do little in the way of evoking improvement, while it often does nothing but harm. Yet punishment cannot always be avoided. How can we punish a child without doing him an injury?

Corporal punishments are to be avoided in any event; they wound the child's sense of honour where it is most sensitive, and give him the feeling that he is defenceless in the hands of a superior person. Against this defencelessness, which he feels to be degrading, the child reacts with the greatest violence. Compensation is the inevitable consequence.

Where blows or other degrading punishments are inflicted as a matter of course the inner protest of the child may be so violent as to result in complete obtuseness. This apathy, which is bound to be followed by the child's failure in any respect, is equivalent to victory all along the line. Passive resistance has long been recognized as the most effective of weapons, to be used against oppression when all other means fail.

Punishments must never be unjust, and never unintelligible to the child; and on no account should they be degrading and humiliating. The child must acknowledge the justice of the penalty, and this he will do only if the punishment follows as the natural consequence of his behaviour. He must learn that for everybody, even for grown-up people, there are laws of general validity; that a prohibition is not issued for the private satisfaction of the teacher, but that there are certain things which one must not do if one wishes to remain a member of the community. Nevertheless, one should think well before announcing prohibitions or penalties. But what is announced (and this refers also to promises) must unconditionally be fulfilled, or the child will receive the impression that the teacher is not to be taken seriously, that he is not to be trusted, or that he himself is not taken seriously. In every particular education must be consistent—but kindly consistent.

After the child has experienced the results of his behaviour, and has had to suffer the consequences, the teacher must quietly and kindly discuss with him the question of making amends for the fault. The child must never have the feeling that the adult is a fault-finder or an enemy; he must always know that in him he has a friend and adviser, who may indeed find certain modes of behaviour wrong and objectionable, but who, on the whole, approves of him and takes him, as a person, seriously.

CHAPTER VI

In the foregoing chapter it was stated that individual-psychology requires ' the education of the teacher '; and it was hinted that the term ' teacher ' must be understood in the widest sense. On the other hand, this requirement is addressed with special urgency to the child's first teacher—to his mother.

Adler proceeds from the standpoint that in all cases where the development of a human being has deviated from the normal the function of the mother—who as the child's first teacher is from the first day of its life the embodiment of the environment—was not properly fulfilled. How has the mother failed in such cases? She has neglected the duty of adjusting the child's attitude toward the community.

The idea of the community assumes a very special importance in individual-psychology. In the first place, as a social structure which contains the multiplicity of individuals; as the arena, so to speak, inside which the conflicts and accommodations of the individual with his fellows take place. Proceeding from the minimum community of mother and child to the community of the family, the individual, growing into wider and wider circles, which are conditioned by human relations, work, interests, religious belief, nationality, etc., becomes a responsible member of the great human community. And in this connexion the notion of the community has for Adler another and a metaphysical significance. He perceives the community as the consummation of human evolution, as the ideal which can never be completely attained, though the efforts and struggles of every individual are directed toward approaching it more closely. The community is perceived as a final goal; the feeling for the community, the attitude toward the community, mark out a path to be followed as the indispensable precondition of all healthy development.

Adler has shown that in all cases of faulty development, in the case of uneducable children and refractory adults, in neuropathic and psychopathic subjects, and even in all persons who have taken to criminal courses, the sense of community has remained undeveloped, or is stunted, or extinguished, making way for the emergence and excessive development of egocentricity. The developed sense of community, on the other hand, regulates the tension between the sense of inferiority and the tendency to compensation, guiding the latter into healthy and positive directions.

Every individual is born with a rudimentary tendency toward solidarity, together with many other possibilities. The sense of solidarity must be fostered, guided and developed by the community, whose first representative, for the child, is the mother; she must take care of the child if it is to live. Many mothers do their utmost for the child as regards caring for its body, yet do not completely fulfil the most important function of the mother, which is that, free of egoism and self-assertion and the appetite for prestige, she should lead the child away from itself, through the narrow family circle, to the greater community. If she does this she will avoid at least one danger. It may often be observed that a woman who has not found satisfaction in her marriage sees in her child the sole meaning and aim of her life; when such an intensive relation develops between mother and child that each of them, jealous and suspicious, wants the other as an exclusive possession, without which life would be impossible; riveting fetters under whose weight she suffers, though she would on no account be without them, because she achieves through them an enormous enhancement of her sense of personality. The mother who fulfils the mother's true function must see to it that she does not remain the only person with whom her child is on intimate terms, and its only assurance. She must make it self-confident and independent of her; for only so is it possible to form individuals capable of making contact with their fellows, capable of solidarity, who find their own foothold inside the community, and do not feel the need of over-assurance or seek it in flight from the community.

When Adler declares that an indissoluble relation exists between the human society and the individual, who is anchored in society, and that this being so, everyone can influence by his behaviour the development of another human being, a new and more significant point of view emerges: the standpoint of responsibility.

In the foregoing chapter it was stated that it is in the power of a human being, irrespective of his physical capacity and organic constitution, irrespective of the influences that impinge upon him from the environment, to function, with all his faculties and possibilities, in accordance with his intelligence; that is, to make free decisions at every moment, thereby assuming responsibility.

The sense of responsibility assumes a central position in the mental structure as conceived by individual-psychology; one must feel responsible for whatever one does in respect of the community. It was stated in an earlier chapter that individual-psychology has *one* orientating standpoint: the standpoint of general utility, utility in the sense of progress, for the community. Thus, on the one hand the behaviour of the individual must be guided by the idea of the service to the community, and on the other hand the community, which consists of individuals, must feel its responsibility for the healthy development of each individual. Most people, however, try more or less to evade responsibility, for they dread nothing so much as defeat and disgrace.

This dread of inadequacy, of finding oneself at the bottom of the ladder, compels the individual to diverge from the normal way, to seek hiding-places, to strive for power and superiority. We have spoken repeatedly of the harmfulness of such behaviour, and individual-psychology has clearly exposed it; but it goes even further, for it tells us that only those can refrain from such behaviour who are courageous enough to refrain.

From this it follows that the basic tendency of pedagogics

and psychotherapy, as conceived by individual-psychology, can be expressed under one common denominator: encouragement—education in courage.

By courage we are not to understand the heroic pose of the man who performs tremendous and hazardous feats. In the sense understood by individual-psychology, to be courageous means: To face up to life with its alternations of joy and sorrow; to make a stand against its cruelties, grappling with them and seeking to overcome them. To be courageous means also to acknowledge one's actions and to accept their consequences; to be able to expose oneself to criticism, to confess to one's errors and failings without feeling oneself disgraced; to be able to change one's course; to be objective, even to be ready—if necessary—sometimes to make oneself disliked; to be able to settle one's own affairs without always having to trouble others with them. To be courageous means, finally, to feel oneself responsible for all that one does in relation to the community.

How can courage be taught?

Even while still at the breast the child should be spared, by method, punctuality and cleanliness, all suspense and anxiety beyond his powers of endurance. He is assured of a quiet unfolding of his faculties only if one restrains oneself, refraining from undue interference, and thereby avoiding mistakes. Above all things one must, as far as is practicable, make it possible for the child to deal for himself with the difficulties by which even a normal development is attended, helping him only where he would otherwise hurt himself. He can be courageous only if he learns at an early stage to overcome resistance, acquiring positive experience, which will help him to develop and make progress. Practice and training, but also the imitation of examples, play a very great part in the development of a child. For this reason it must never be forgotten that the behaviour of every individual, whether he has or has not any direct dealings with children, is not without effect; that the adults of to-day were the children of yesterday, and that the children of to-day will be the adults of to-morrow, who will have to influence and educate children. Of course, the personality of the individual in charge of the child's earliest education, who has to give it its first and most essential orientation, is of the very greatest importance; since it has to exhale the atmosphere of matter-of-fact security. The child must learn by experience that even in painful and unpleasant situations this person does not shuffle or prevaricate, and does not tell untruths, but submits to the same objective laws which he or she requires the child to obey.

All the mistakes of a too indulgent, or unloving, or too strict and inconsequent education, which lead to effeminacy, dependence on others, embitterment, and insensibility, or fill the child with uncertainty and suspicion, must be as far as possible avoided. The child cannot be too carefully guarded against all humiliating and embarrassing situations. But it is never too early to teach the child to have consideration for those about him, and to require him to have the same regard for the persons and rights of his fellows as is claimed for his own person and his own rights. Here he must be made to realize that every individual represents a link of an infinitely long chain, and that he has to make to this chain whatever contribution is within his powers. Only in this way can the child acquire the sense of 'belonging,' of solidarity, and with that, the feeling of self-confidence; only thus can he learn that he can feel himself to be of value only if he makes himself of value to others. Then it will no longer be necessary to compensate the sense of inferiority by spurious and unprofitable expedients.

Adler has divided the whole complex of the problems which confront a human being into three parts: the problem relating to one's neighbours (the relation of the individual to his fellows), the problem of vocation (the relation of the individual to work), and the erotic problem (the relation to the sexual partner). Of course, the whole constitutes a circular problem whose various sectors represent only separate divisions of the one great social problem. The truly socially-minded individual—that is, the human being with a sense of community, of solidarity—will tackle all life's problems with courage, whether they concern his relations to his family, his friends, or his work, or his love affairs.

The pedagogy of the future must be capable of so preparing the individual that he will be able to solve the social problems (and all life's problems are social problems) in a satisfactory and generally profitable manner. How inadequate this preparation has been hitherto is shown by the number of unwilling, psychopathic, ailing individuals, and also by the happenings in the world at large. This is why it is so essential that Adler's doctrine should become more widely known, so that all those who are interested in the healing of our ailing age, in the creation of a new and healthy humanity, can co-operate in the task.

Sound development is possible only if all the powers latent in the child are free to unfold themselves; only if the child is taught to be courageous, to feel responsible for his action, to feel himself one of a community. Courage, the sense of responsibility, the sense of solidarity; they all merge into one another, and they are present when a human being acts 'reasonably,' in Adler's sense of the word. Adler has told us that by 'reason' he means 'commonsense'; the sense of all forms of expression, the content of all modes of behaviour which may be counted as beneficial to the community—that is, as generally serviceable.

Conclusion

Proceeding from the fact that it is necessary to foster and extend our understanding of human nature, an attempt was made in the foregoing chapter to outline the fundamental ideas of individual-psychology, and in so doing to show what important progress in the knowledge and understanding of the human personality must be credited to this doctrine. But it is not enough to indicate the line to be followed in the investigation and comprehension of human nature; for inherent in the doctrine is the inexorable demand for self-knowledge, which is indeed the precondition of all fruitful inquiry. When Adler stipulates for the education of the educator, when he comes to the conclusion that regardless of the physical and organic constitution, regardless of the environmental influences, the individual is capable of functioning in accordance with his intelligence, he always emphasizes the fact that the individual must know himself in respect of his positive and negative qualities. In respect of his positive qualities, in order that all the valuable possibilities and capacities dormant in him may be brought to their highest development, and thereby contribute to the general progress; in respect of his negative qualities, in order that he may abandon defective attitudes and modes of behaviour, and effect a readjustment. For what distinguishes man from all other living creatures is the possession of an intellect capable of considering and weighing, and also the capacity for intuition and sympathy. Only in so far as he uses these gifts rightly—in relation to the generally accepted values of humanity—and allows his willing and acting to be determined by them—can he give his life a meaning and show himself worthy of his human status.

If we once more examine the psychic structure of Adler's doctrine we shall find:

1. It proceeds from the investigation of the physical and organic constitution (biological basis).
2. It investigates the psychic conditions under which an individual acts or refrains from action (psychological working method).
3. It takes the human being in contact with his fellows as the object of its researches (sociological method of approach).
4. It endeavours to attribute a meaning to human existence (metaphysical standpoint).

It is obvious, then, that individual-psychology has overstepped the limits of simple psychology[1]; in fact, that it represents:

[1] Dr. Alexander Müller.

A doctrine of the human being in his physical and psychic totality, in his contact with reality, and his longing for a significant form of life.

Reverence for life in its creative power and the multiplicity of its phenomenal forms, the basic idea of evolution, the unfaltering conviction of the freedom of the human personality (within the limitations of cosmic laws), the sturdy optimism and the warm humanity which distinguish Adler's work, ought to be capable, together with the unconditional requirements inherent in them, of building up a new man, once more conscious of the dignity of his human status. By so doing it would give the world a different countenance.

The doctrine of individual-psychology is evidence that its leading idea—to make a contribution to the progress of humanity—has been nobly realized by its creator, Alfred Adler.

PRACTICE

I

A Child who falls on her knees

I SAW Gretchen and her mother for the first time in the waiting-room of a doctor who had advised me that the first case for individual-psychological treatment had been transferred from the psychiatrical clinic of a district authority.

Gretchen was a tall, very well-developed girl, and very pretty; I guessed her to be about fourteen. Her mother, still young, and very fragile, apparently of proletarian origin, opened the conversation. Did I know the doctor?—was he nice, was he young or old, fair or dark? The woman seemed herself to find these questions rather embarrassing, for she excused herself, in some confusion, by explaining that her daughter was terribly afraid of doctors. Our conversation was interrupted by the opening of the consulting-room door, and I received from the doctor the introductory report from the clinic. It was as follows:

> Gretchen has been suffering for about three months from a functional weakness of the musculature of the thigh and calf, which manifests itself in frequent giving way at the knees—so that she falls on her knees—whether walking or standing—twenty to thirty times a day.[1] The most varied treatments have been applied: orthopædic, electrical, thermal (hot air), massage; but without result. The child's great irritability and sensitiveness are conspicuous. It has been decided that a psychic treatment should be attempted. Report requested.

[1] The clinical picture reminds one emphatically of the cases of *affective loss of tonus* described in particular by Redlich, which are included in the wider morphographic category of *narcolepsy*.

In affective loss of tonus it is usual for any kind of muscular relaxation to occur after emotional excitement, leading in some cases to falling to the ground, in less serious cases to a sudden giving at the knees, or the dropping of one limb, as a rule without loss of consciousness. (For this suggestion I have to thank Dr. Alexandra Adler, Boston, and Dr. Ernst Haase, formerly of Berlin.)

And now the preliminary history, which I learned, to some extent, during consultation with the doctor, supplementing my knowledge by a subsequent interview with the girl's mother in her own house:

Gretchen is not 14, as I thought, but 12½. She was born on New Year's Eve, 1914, the first and only child of her parents, a few days after her father was killed. The father had been foreman in a factory; the mother, at the time of the child's birth, was staying with her mother, who had a small business in a little country town not far from Hamburg. One can imagine the mother's troubles and anxieties during the last few days preceding the child's birth, and into what an atmosphere of mourning and hopelessness the child was born; further, one can assume that this fatherless child was much petted and spoiled by her mother and grandmother. She was a healthy and unusually pretty child.

When she was one year old she was taken to Berlin by her mother, who obtained a job in a factory. She put Gretchen out to board, but only for six months, as it was evident that the child was not being properly looked after, and was not developing physically. She then took care of the child herself, leaving her during the day with friendly neighbours, and attending to her after her day's work. So Gretchen grew up, a pretty, lovable child, whom everybody was glad to see, and so about two years went by, during which her mother, except when she was at work, devoted herself entirely to the child. Gretchen was now just over four years of age. In the same building there was a restaurant in which she spent much of her time, already making herself useful. An habitual customer, an elderly man, took a particular interest in the pretty child, and through Gretchen he made her mother's acquaintance. This man, who was also a foreman in a factory, was a foreigner, and seemed rather lonely. After some time a relation developed between him and Gretchen's mother, and they lived together. They could not marry; apparently because the man was a Swiss citizen, and his papers were not in order. As a matter of fact, they were legally married only a year before I made Gretchen's acquaintance; however, the mother did not believe that this irregular situation had troubled the child in any way.

In the meantime Gretchen had acquired a brother—now aged 5—and a sister—now aged 2. She was greatly attached to her parents, especially to her father, and was very glad to have a brother and sister, though she often wanted to dominate them.

At the age of 6 Gretchen went to school. She was very glad to do so, and at first all went well. When she had been at school a fortnight she was run over by a motor-car and badly injured. She sustained fractures of the femur and the tibia, as well as a severe head injury, and was some months in hospital. When at last she was sufficiently recovered to leave the hospital she contracted pyelitis and catarrh of the bladder, which again necessitated prolonged treatment; after a total period of about a year she again left the hospital. At first she was greatly intimidated by the traffic in the streets; but after a month in the country this nervousness gradually diminished. But another trouble made its appearance: the child suddenly began to suffer from enuresis (bed-wetting).

When we reflect that Gretchen, the pretty, lovable child, who had had so much to suffer, was petted by the doctors and nurses of the hospital, and by her parents, when they came to see her, one can imagine that now, on her return home, she expected once more to be the centre of attention. But this was impossible, for it was just about this time that her little brother arrived, to claim his mother's especial care. The bed-wetting was thus to be interpreted as the unconscious attempt to imitate the newly-born child, and in this way to compel the mother to give her also special attention.

The means adopted by the child were determined by the 'somatic preparedness' of the sensitive urinary organ, which registered the psychic disturbance. The bed-wetting continued for about three years; it disappeared when another symptom developed; pains in the region of the waist, for which no cause could be discovered, and which continued for about a year.

At the age of 11 she asked her mother whether children were really brought by the stork. Her mother then enlightened her, warning her that a girl must guard herself carefully, and must never let herself be seen or touched by a man, excepting the man she was going to marry.

Some time afterwards Gretchen was admitted to hospital as a suspected case of diphtheria and typhus. There was a young doctor there, who paid her a great deal of attention, played with her during his time off duty, embraced her, called her 'his little wife,' and finally made a genital examination. That same afternoon the mother came to the hospital and found the child greatly upset; her mother had told her that she must never let a man touch her, etc. The objection that this warning could never refer to a doctor, who must always do whatever is necessary, did nothing to calm the child. She demanded urgently that she must be allowed to leave the hospital, and her mother was able to comply with her wish, as that very day a report had been received to the effect that the examination had yielded negative results. Gretchen could not be induced to bid the doctor good-bye, and her mother informed me that she had not told her husband anything about this affair, for in such matters he was particularly touchy. The young doctor, by the way, was exceptionally dark in complexion, which explains the mother's inquiry, in the waiting-room, as to whether the doctor was by any chance dark, for in that case Gretchen would have been particularly timid and shy of him.

When she came home again she showed signs of extreme anxiety; she would not be left in the flat, unless her brother and sister were there; she refused to go into the street in the dark, and was always afraid of men.

Some time after this her father fell seriously ill with diabetes; for months he was in hospital. In the meantime —it was now spring—her mother contracted influenza, followed by pulmonary catarrh. Gretchen was greatly distressed, and one day asked her mother: what am I to do if you both die? (It is interesting to note the form of the question.) It was about this time that Gretchen's symptom first made its appearance.

Her mother told me that Gretchen is a good scholar, but has special difficulties with her arithmetic. The arithmetic master is very strict, and strikes the children; he has not struck her yet, he has only once pulled her ear, but since then she so dreads the arithmetic lesson that she can't do anything.

When I called on her, the mother complained of the child's extreme sensitiveness and irritability, and she added, weeping, that Gretchen refused in a very nasty way to help her with the housework, and altogether did not realize the difficulty of their situation. This complaint was in contradiction to the mother's statement when she visited the doctor —that the child was a joy to her parents, and their only anxiety was her ' illness.'

It was naturally interesting to learn when—in what situation—the symptom first made its appearance. After prolonged inquiry I elicited the following: the symptom began to make its appearance while the mother was ill, and it first occurred in school. The children had had an arithmetic lesson—that is, the subject which Gretchen particularly dreaded—and this was followed by a German class, taken by a mistress of whom Gretchen was particularly fond. During this lesson Gretchen had talked to her neighbour, for which the teacher reprimanded her sharply, and as a punishment she was moved to the front bench; but the teacher did not reprimand the other child. While most of the children in this class came from very poor families, the other girl came from a rather better home. The two children were ' friends,' but there was keen rivalry between them. Gretchen could not get over the teacher's injustice; she felt her behaviour to be a betrayal, for she loved the teacher dearly, and had always thought that the teacher was fond of her. In the break following this class Gretchen had ' slipped up '; that is, for the first time she had fallen on her knees, and from this time onwards the symptom persisted.

Since the giving way at the knees (falling and remaining only for a moment on the knees) was quite involuntary—whether the child was standing or walking—it was a very disquieting symptom. The child was taken to the doctor (as the child of a father who had fallen in the war she came under the special welfare scheme), but he could not make much of the case, and after all sorts of treatments, as already described, had been tried without result, the child was at last sent to the psychiatrical clinic, and was finally transferred to me for treatment.

As we have seen, the first step in individual-psychological treatment is to ascertain the patient's ' style ' of life (because without the knowledge of the individual dynamic law one cannot understand the patient, and therefore cannot help him or her), in which connexion reminiscences, dreams, and fantasies afford one significant hints.

When I asked Gretchen for some reminiscence of her very early childhood she could at first think of nothing. Suddenly there came into her mind a recollection from her second year, or so she believed. It was this: She was taken to see her grandmother in the little country town of which she was so fond. Next door to her grandmother's house was a butcher's shop, and since the two families were on friendly terms the little girl was often in the shop. One day " a lamb, a curly lamb was brought in, and suddenly the butcher took up a hammer and . . ." To my query, " Well, and . . . ? " the child replied, " I don't know any more "; and she said, shaking herself, " it was horrible! " What was so horrible there was no need to explain. The ' curly lamb,' a wether, was struck on the head by the butcher's hammer; and what happens when a wether is struck on the head? Its forelegs give way at the knees!

This reminiscence, which told me a great deal, was put aside for the time being, and we began to discuss the child's daily life. This afforded some material, for characteristic symptoms revealed themselves; extreme timidity, sensitiveness, dread of the arithmetic lesson, fear of disgracing herself, ambition, rivalry with other children, rebellion against the mother if she made any demands on the child, attempts to dominate the younger children, a love of fine clothes, and complaints that she could not keep up with richer pupils as she would like; that is, a feeling of social inferiority.

Gretchen's attempts to centre attention upon her symptom were treated lightly; the chief emphasis was laid on the child's mode of behaviour and its analysis. It appeared that she was perfectly willing to help her mother to wash up or dry the dishes, etc., but only if she felt inclined; not when she was asked to do so; and that she could not bear to have her mother make little of her services. It sometimes happened that the child would sweep a room of her own accord, and take pleasure in doing it, and that afterwards her mother would criticize her performance. She could not bear that; she would rather do nothing at all! It was necessary to make the child understand her mother's position, to show her how overworked the woman was, and what a problem she, Gretchen, presented. It was also necessary, of course, to speak to the mother, and to get her to understand that she must help to enable the child to take pleasure in her work, by acknowledging her efforts; she must not detract from her inclination to work by blaming her, but must gradually show her what she could perhaps do better.

At first Gretchen was unable to recall a dream; she could remember only one, which she had dreamed some time ago, and which had frightened her greatly. It appeared that she had dreamed it at the time when her mother was ill, and that this was the time when the symptom first appeared.

> " I was sitting (she said) on the outer window-sill of our house (a four-story tenement house) and looking through the closed window into the room, which was empty. Then the door opened and five tall black men came in, with tall black hats, thick black cloaks, and great black shoes. I

was so startled that I fell from the window-sill into the courtyard, which was covered all over with broken glass. I woke with pains all over my body."

What did this dream mean? She was sitting on the outer window-sill; that is, she was in a very exposed position. The window was closed, whereby her isolation was still further emphasized; moreover, the room was empty, so her parents were absent. Where were they? The appearance of the black men, such men as she may often have seen in the street when funeral processions were passing, gives us the answer: the child was anticipating the death of her parents. Her parents dead, she finds herself in an exposed—that is, a responsible—position (as the eldest); but this is too much; she would surely break down; so she falls into the courtyard. Simultaneously with the appearance of the black men she remembers the painful experience with the young doctor, which had brought her down to earth unexpectedly. The dream really repeats the question: What am I to do if you both die? (she does not ask, What are *we* to do?) and at the same time it supplies a commentary to the recollection of the 'curly lamb'; if things are too difficult, then one doesn't go on; one just falls down; or one gives way at the knees. It is only here that an allusion is made to this recollection, which the child now understands.

It was necessary to explain matters at the school. The teacher had told the children, who saw that Gretchen had to keep on staying away from school on account of her medical treatment: "You must be careful with Gretchen because, you know, she is ill."

The schoolmistress had also to be asked to refrain from allowing Gretchen to assume a special position in the school on account of her 'illness,' but to treat her just as she treated the other children. The mathematical master, too, was requested, in a friendly manner, to deal very cautiously with the child, as she had endured a great deal of physical suffering, and was extremely nervous and easily frightened; and it was hinted that by manifesting special interest and goodwill he might be of great assistance. Both teachers did their best to comply with these requests; and now one had to try to encourage Gretchen to the point of making another attempt to follow the classes in arithmetic. She found, at the same time, that the master was particularly kind to her, so that she gradually gained confidence and was able to do better. Her mother too behaved sensibly, so that here too the child found that her former attitude was mistaken, and that the mode of behaviour recommended was the right one.

The little manifestations of jealousy in respect of her friends were discussed, and the attempts at dominance by which she sought to achieve what was otherwise beyond her power. She also confided to me that she was miserable when a friend was given a new woollen jacket, such as she herself had so longed to possess. Here one could assure her that such things were relative—that her friend might long to possess things which she could not obtain, and which she admired on others. The only way of gradually obtaining what one longs for was to work, and to behave to other people in such a way as to gain the appreciation which she so ardently desired. Gretchen followed this lecture very intelligently, and made an effort to discipline herself in the direction indicated.

Although I made light of her symptom, Gretchen kept on telling me how often her knees had given way in the course of the day, and gradually a progressive subsidence of the trouble was perceptible. Twice there was a slight recurrence; once, when during a swimming lesson she was unexpectedly left to support herself, and swallowed some water; and again, when her father's hope of obtaining a post as foreman in the little town in which her grandmother was living had to be abandoned, by reason of his age. However, the recurrence of the symptom was in each case only temporary. Here is a dream which she had while she was making progress:

> The children at school tell her that she will have to go into hospital again on account of her giving at the knees;

she is terribly afraid and wakes with this feeling of anxiety. She also considers, in the dream, whether she shall continue the course which she is now following (entailing hard work and co-operation) or whether she shall relapse into irresponsibility (illness). Her anxiety, her fear of being ill, shows that she has already taken her decision.

Here is a waking phantasy; or, as she put it, a dream she had without being asleep: she had a business, like her grandmother, but with a girl assistant in the shop, and help in the house. Here we see an expression of the child's longing for a higher social position, and also the wish for subordinates—that is, the wish to exert domination.

After six weeks' treatments, at the beginning of the summer holidays, the psychiatrical clinic was advised of the patient's progress and asked whether the treatment should be continued after the holidays. Since the reply was in the affirmative, the visits were resumed six weeks later. At the last interview before the holidays I had occasion once more to point to the harmful consequences of her incorrect training, and to show, by the successful results already obtained, that the attitude which she had now achieved, and which she must practise further, was the correct one.

After the end of the holidays, and before the beginning of further treatment, a further inquiry was made of the psychiatrical clinic. It was established that the symptom had entirely disappeared, while the irritability and susceptibility were greatly diminished, and the child was now endeavouring in every way to fall into line and co-operate with others. Consequently further treatment was not considered necessary. Some misgiving was still felt that a relapse might occur if the newly-acquired ideas were not sufficiently established. Fortunately this was not the case. Subsequent inquiries, over a period of about two years, elicited the fact that the child had passed the beginning of menstruation without disturbance, and was now developing normally.

Now for a personal estimate:

Gretchen is a delicate and cossetted child, who found it easy, by her pleasing appearance and her amiability, to win people's affection; that is, to be 'on top.' But she was willing to co-operate only for so long as no difficulties presented themselves. The accident which she sustained was for her a great shock; on the other hand, as she was still more petted and pampered, it intensified her sense of personality. When she came home again, to everyday life, and moreover, found herself, in her own opinion, relegated to an inferior position by the birth of her brother, she had (unconsciously) to adopt other methods in order to draw special attention to herself. Here she was assisted by the susceptibility of her urinary organs (enuresis, girdle pains). Her startling experience in hospital helped to increase her anxiety, which finally sought to impress others into her service; she could not be left alone in the house, and would not go out into the streets after dark.

In her quality of pampered child her individual dynamic law bade her feel that the claims which others made upon her were excessive; she did not like to be given orders or instructions, and complied with them only if she was pleased to do so. She felt any reprimand as a disgrace. The fact that the schoolmistress punished *her* and not her friend proved that people were unjust and unkind, since spoilt children always want more than they receive, are always discontented with what they get, and always seem to themselves ill-treated. Such children are always intent on seeking assurance for their ego and take little interest in others. The symptom of giving way at the knees made its appearance when Gretchen, by the supposed discovery that her teacher felt less affection for her than for her friend, had suffered a serious defeat; and this happened just about the time when, owing to her father's illness and unemployment, and her mother's illness, she felt her personal security to be threatened by the possible loss of her parents.

The childish experience with the 'curly lamb,' in its horror, furnished the cliché, the pattern of behaviour to be adopted in a tight place, in a moment of distress, when fate deals one a blow on the head; there is nothing for it then but to collapse. To do this Gretchen had (of course, unconsciously) to bring her organic inadequacy, the injury to her innervation and musculature resulting from her motor-car accident, under psychic control. Her aim was—to be right 'on top.' Perhaps she achieved a concrete representation of this position in the idea of the well-fed townsman with his business and his employees, who has always to look askance at other people and compare himself with them.

When it became clear to Gretchen that one must not collapse in difficult situations, but that one can overcome them; that the appreciation she so desired must be won, not by illness and the avoidance of work, but by effort and co-operation, she no longer had need of her symptom. She was ready to alter her mode of behaviour in accordance with her newly-acquired ideas, so that before long she was cured.

II

The Silent Child

ANNE was $7\frac{1}{4}$ years of age when she was brought to the psychological clinic at the central Welfare Office.

As the mother and child entered the room they presented a curious spectacle. One saw a frail little woman, tightly embraced by a delicate little girl, who did not show her face, but had buried her head in her mother's clothes. It was as though only one peculiar and rather misshapen creature was entering the room. Despite all encouragement, Anne could not be persuaded to raise her head, and the mother began her report:

Anne was suffering from an impediment of speech; that is, she *could* speak quite well and correctly, but she *would* speak to no one but her mother and her sister, a year and nine months her junior; she could not look people in the face and would not give them her hand.

This was the previous history of the case:

Anne was the eldest child; she had, as has been stated, a younger sister. Extremely delicate at birth, Anne was fed from the breast for seven months. In the first six weeks of her life the child had no regular movements of the bowels; recourse was had to medicines and massage. From the second week until well on into the second year of her life Anne suffered from extreme restlessness and convulsive movements which kept her awake at night. Her mother often had to hold her little arms and legs for an hour or longer until the child lay quiet. After sleeping for a little while she would wake, and the whole trouble would begin anew.

The father, who was formerly a railway employee, was severely wounded in the first world war, and was in receipt of a small pension. He was now employed in a hairdresser's shop. This nervous and ailing man naturally needed his night's rest; it angered him to have it disturbed, and he scolded the child loudly.

At one year Anne was able to walk; at fifteen months she could speak; but she then gave proof that she had been perfectly sensible of her father's nightly outbursts of anger, for she spoke only to her mother; she simply boycotted her father, and refused to speak to him. When her sister was born—a strong and very healthy child—Anne was at first extremely shy of her; but later on she spoke to her and played with her; however, she did not care for company, but was very well able to amuse herself. As a very young child she had whooping-cough, measles, and mumps.

Her shyness became more and more conspicuous; she spoke to no one, turned away if addressed, and would not give her hand to any one. But she spoke incessantly when she was alone with her mother, so that the latter often found her volubility exhausting. Her mother reflected that many children are shy, and thought that Anne's peculiar behaviour would cease when she attended school. At the age of $6\frac{1}{4}$ she was sent to school. Her mother accompanied her to the school, and while other children cried and clung to their mothers, and were unwilling to let them go, Anne sat rigid and immovable in her place, answered no questions, stared straight in front of her, and allowed her mother to leave her. The school doctor told the mother that this was not a case of ordinary shyness, but that the child's attitude was abnormal. She was not to come to school for another year. In the meantime he advised her mother to send her to a kindergarten.

Anne was now sent to a large kindergarten in the city. She was there for ten months, and in all that time she never once took part, by word or movement, in the activities of the other children; she sat silent and motionless, never co-operating with the others. Then she was taken to school for the second time, and her mother was painfully anxious as to the outcome.

While her case was being described Anne persisted, at first, in the same behaviour as when she first entered the clinic. Still turning her back, she gradually rubbed her head upwards against her mother's body. Her mother had opened her cloak; her dress had a V-shaped neck. Anne moved her head upwards until she had reached the V-shaped opening, when she sucked at her mother's throat, as though pretending to be a suckling.

It was decided that the child should be subjected to treatment. I professed myself ready to make the experiment. When the mother was about to leave it was only with difficulty that the child was detached from her body. After much sighing and groaning from the mother, " Oh, it's dreadful to see the child! " etc., the girl was induced to stand up. At first she turned her face away; but when she could do so no longer, one saw that her delicate little face was extremely pale; her eyes were closed. When her mother took her hand in order to leave the room with her it seemed as though the child was unable to walk; she staggered from one leg to the other. So she was not only the dumb child, but also the blind and lame child.

Before Anne came to me I had another talk with the mother. I made her realize that since Anne had been a very sick child, and was still very delicate and weakly, she must of course have been greatly concerned about her, and this would naturally have the effect of making the child very dependent and lacking in self-confidence. She had removed all obstacles from her path, had done everything for her, and had even answered for her when the child was questioned, so that she had no need to speak. Since the little girl never had any opportunity of coping with difficulties independently, she had grown so accustomed to leaving everything to her mother that now she did not venture to do anything of her own accord, being afraid that without her mother she would never be able to do it. Anxiety, too, was very largely at the bottom of her impediment of speech. The problem now was to give the child courage, and the mother could help to do this if she would endeavour, very lovingly, but quite firmly, to detach the child a little from her person; if she would try to prevent the child from clinging to her; if she would give her little tasks about the house and send her on little errands, always thanking her if she did them properly, in order to give her more self-confidence. All this the mother understood perfectly, and she agreed to do her best.

On the occasion of the child's first visit I had set up some toys in the consulting-room. The mother came in with the child; Anne once again tried to creep under her cloak, and clung to her when she wanted to go. I had to separate them gently before the mother could take her departure. Again the child refused to let me see her face, turned her back to me, and for some time stood motionless, her fists pressed convulsively to her eyes. I spoke, sang, and whistled to myself, drummed on the table with my hands, and moved about noisily; then the child was taken home. On the next visit she persisted in the same motionless attitude, with this difference, that she let her arms hang at her side; she stared at the wall, without turning round. I behaved as on the previous occasion, perhaps more noisily. On her next visit she reacted to my noisy behaviour in so far as she sometimes plucked nervously at her pinafore, while remaining in the same position as before.

Hitherto, when she arrived, I had always helped her off with her coat; this she allowed me to do, with averted face. Now I made the experiment of helping to remove one arm only from its sleeve. She actually remained in the same position, with her coat half off, during the hour of her visit, while the next time she turned her head very slightly, but, of course, not so far that I could see her face. I had asked the mother not to enter the room any longer on coming and leaving. On coming to take the child home she was to call out, asking Anne to leave the room for the entrance-hall; measuring the time with my watch, I found the child took two minutes to cover a distance of ten feet. When I put a chair on the spot on the carpet which Anne had selected for standing on, the child moved a step farther and remained with her back turned to me. I was able to observe that when the telephone bell rang shrilly about eight feet behind her the child did not make the least movement. Now, on my advice, the mother, when she came to fetch the child, did not enter the flat, but standing outside the entrance door called to the girl through the open door of the room. At first Anne took no notice of her, and she did not react until her mother, after calling her several times in vain, observed (as we had previously agreed), " In the meantime I'm going on; no doubt you'll follow me." When she turned as though she were really going Anne very quickly ran after her.

All this time I had spoken to Anne without receiving any answer; I had sung, drummed on the table, whistled.

On account of illness the mother had to interrupt her visits.

In the meantime Anne was sent to school, where she behaved, of course, with absolute passivity.

When she came to me again after an eight weeks' interval she was just as shy as ever, with the difference that she now chose another spot to stand on. She now crept into a corner of the room, pressing herself into it with her hands covering her face.

The mother had always appeared with the child quite punctually. Once, when she was late, she explained that she always left home much earlier than was necessary, as she always had to interrupt their journey, because Anne had a fit of nausea and vomiting on the way. To-day it had been very bad; they had had to get out twice; that was why they were late.

When Anne had gone to her corner again I began to play with a little ball, throwing it against her back. After some time I noted a tiny movement of the rigid body, and looking down on her from behind I could see on her cheek the suggestion of a faint smile. On her next visit she remained standing in her corner and did not react in any way to my game with the ball. At last I pulled her out of the corner, throwing her from one arm to the other, saying, " Out of the corner, into the corner! " until I noted that the iron tension of the body was relaxing a little, and again I saw a surreptitious smile. Next time I began with the gymnastic performance, swinging her in and out of the corner, until she became more relaxed, and even laughed. She still took her place in the corner, but she was on the whole more relaxed, and was ready to laugh, but still always with averted face.

After many experiments with the ball she was at last induced to show some activity, in a negative sense. While bouncing the ball against her back I began to speak to myself, " Well, this is a reliable wall, a wall I can rely on; at all events it doesn't move." Whereupon she took a step to one side, still turning her back to me. Gradually her wanderings extended all over the room. She became active; she began to move the chairs and other pieces of furniture, and took little pictures within her reach off the wall, still reacting to everything in a negative manner.

I had, of course, to get into touch with her school-teacher. She told me that Anne never spoke a word, and did not respond to any request; but when her teacher took her copybook from her satchel she began to write with the other children, and then her work was the best in the class. I explained the mechanism of the child's inhibition of speech to the teacher; it resulted from a lack of self-confidence; and I begged her not to lose patience. She gave me her promise, adding that no child had ever so taxed her patience. She also told me that the other children were intensely interested in Anne, helping her in every way and struggling for the privilege of sitting beside her. (It should be observed that Anne was always conspicuously well dressed, as her mother made all her clothes for her.) In the class she was known as ' the dumb girl.'

Our gymnastic performances had gradually become little scuffles, which amused Anne greatly; it turned out that she had a great sense of fun, and before long she was shouting and screaming. Once, when I asked her a question, she replied with a loud derisive laugh.

I now heard from the teacher that at the end of the spring term Anne would have to leave the school, since there was a rule that children who had not spoken for three months had to leave; they could then go to a special school. An application was made to the Board of Education, in which the case was described, and in which reference was made to the treatment which the child was receiving; with the result that permission was granted for the child to remain at the school for the time being.

On her last visit before the summer vacation Anne inadvertently uttered a word—and was greatly startled. It is not surprising that the word was 'No.' I took no notice of it.

Her mother told me that Anne had begged her to inquire as to my address during the holidays, as she would like to write to me. She did send me two post cards—very nicely written, considering her circumstances—which were to be regarded as the first attempts to emerge from her congealed self-preoccupation.

In the middle of August Anne's visits were resumed after an interval of some eight weeks. At first she was again very shy; but she soon became active once more, romping about, crowing and shrieking; she was noisy and vigorous. After she had paid me a few visits she was unwell, and there was a further interval of three weeks. Her mother told me that children from the school came to see her (as they had done before this), and that she sat beside them like a little princess, without speaking, while the others chattered.

When Anne came to see me again she was once more extremely reserved; and then I did something that was not quite in accordance with the method of individual-psychology —I spoke to her about her symptoms, more or less in the following words: "You know, of course, why you are coming to me; because you don't speak to any one except your mother and sister. I am going to tell you why you are behaving like this. Your mother has always done everything you wanted her to do; you have always been like a little princess, who had only to give orders. But this goes down only with your mother and your little sister, who also does whatever you want her to do. When you meet other people you are afraid you can't go on being a princess, and you would rather not say anything at all, for you couldn't bear to feel that other people are not your servants. And that's how it is at school. But I think you are making a mistake! You can write better and you are better at arithmetic than the other children, and you would find, if you would speak, that there's no need to be a princess, and that other people needn't always do as one wishes; but that it's much nicer to do something together with them—to work with them and talk with them, to play and laugh with them. So, just think it over!"

During this speech Anne crouched behind a chair, peeping out from time to time with a hostile expression. She had a pondering look, such as an adult may wear when considering some very difficult problem. Her attitude toward me was negative.

Her mother told me again that the other children were still coming to see Anne, and that the day before Anne had whispered a word for the first time. This was just after my advice to her. Further, her mother was able to assure me that in accordance with our experiment she had been trying harder than ever to draw the child out of herself a little; she had even got her to go on little errands—for example, to go into the shops while her mother waited outside. She had a hard struggle at first, but now she had come to the point of going into the shops and whispering a few words which she had committed to memory; but if she was then asked any question she did not reply. After the child had come to see me three or four times in the week I allowed her to come daily.

Now I began to throw dice. Before this Anne could never be induced to play games, but now she joined me, following my instructions, ruling two columns on a sheet of paper, and writing down the results of the throws. She did this with great accuracy, and wrote down my results also. But this is how she did it: after every throw she crept with her paper and pencil under the table, which was covered with a cloth, lay down on her stomach, carefully entered the result, and then came up again. So she had not as yet the courage to confess to herself that she was willing to co-operate. She did the totting up also under the table, and succeeded in adding up totals exceeding 100, although at school she had only counted up to 20.

Before this, when we were playing together with a ball, and the ball fell to the ground, she could not at first be persuaded to pick it up; she would then roll the ball towards her with her feet, and lift it up with her feet. After we had busied ourselves with the dice for some time she had so far improved that if requested she would immediately pick up a fallen object with her hand.

Early in October I invited a very nice child to join us; she was of the same age as Anne, and was staying with an acquaintance of mine. I left the children together. Anne crowed and romped about, but could not be persuaded to speak or play. During this period I once made the experiment of allowing her to meet the other child on a playground. The other little girl tried her very best, but there was nothing to be done with Anne; she was intolerable, and would not join her companion in anything. At a second visit, on the following day, she was familiar in her manner; she laughed and romped with the other child, but did not speak.

In the meantime she had again adopted an extremely negative attitude toward me; I spoke to her again with reference to her playing the princess; I told her it was very boring, and that I at all events was not going to place myself at her service. The result was at first a return of the hostile attitude, but then she altered her tactics; she was very noisy, romping and barking; now for the first time she uttered inarticulate sounds.

In the middle of October I one day showed her a card which she had sent me during the holidays, and asked her to read it to me. Of course, she did not do so, and I deplored her refusal, for she could see, from the fact that I had kept the card, how pleased I had been to receive it. She then began some articulate conversational exercises, in which I accompanied her. Then, in a babyish tone, came the word 'Hamma,' and when I asked, "Do you mean Mamma?" she repeated, laughing, several times, 'Hamma,' and at last, loudly and clearly, uttered the word 'Hampelmann.'[1] Whether she meant that I, whom she was leading such a dance, was the Jumping Jack, or whether it was she who was giving such a performance, I could not ascertain. When her mother came to fetch her, Anne, as usual, did not speak, but indicated by gestures what she wanted.

On other occasions she was quiet at first, until I uttered the password 'Hampelmann'; then she began to put babyish words together; they were without meaning, but she laughed and was full of fun. The noteworthy fact was that in her comedy she unconsciously followed the development of the growing child, inasmuch as she spoke now only in infinitives, and then merely repeated "I, I, I." Another time she pulled me about, saying, "*Tomm, mietommen, pielen*" (baby language, as it were, "Tum, tum wiv me, p'ay"). I entered into the game; the child must be taught to speak; she must pay close attention and watch my lips, and I would now repeat the numbers. I began slowly and solemnly, "One!" She looked at me mockingly and said, at once, loudly and plainly, "Two!" I regretted that she had not paid attention. I would repeat the number again; again she gave me the same derisive glance, and even more clearly than before she cried "Three!" In this way I let her say the numbers up to 10, which she did, teasingly, with laughter.

On the next occasion it pleased her to do nothing at all. At this I told her that I had no intention of boring myself;

[1] Jumping Jack.

and I took up a book. She pulled at me, but did not speak.

Another time we threw dice; she was to tell me the results; she did so in a whisper. About this time I asked her mother whether she still had attacks of nausea and vomiting on the way to the clinic. The woman, with whom I had often discussed the child and her behaviour, was quite surprised by my question; these symptoms had entirely disappeared some time ago.

We 'played at school.' Anne dictated letters of the alphabet to me; she had to pronounce them first, which she did in an abrupt whisper; I had to repeat them, and was then given marks; of course, always bad ones.

Another time she brought her doll with her, wrote the name 'Susi' for me, and even spoke it in a whisper; then we both 'played at school' with the doll. She spoke for the doll, in a babyish tone, but more loudly and clearly than when she was answering for herself. Another day she brought her spelling-book from her school. She made me read, and she herself read in a whisper; then she switched off the light—a thing she was fond of doing—and repeated by heart the letters and syllables of the first lesson. This was a great joke to her, and she spoke loudly and plainly. When the light was switched on she spoke in whispers again, but coherently. This was the first day on which she spoke to me in front of her mother, and to her mother in front of me, though she only whispered a few words.

Another day she was rowdy from the first, pulling me from one chair to another, speaking hoarsely in baby language, and then loudly and coherently; she babbled all through her visit, now and again throwing herself down on the sofa, trampling and shrieking, and behaving as though she were intoxicated; but when her mother came for her she only whispered. Another time, when she was not quite herself, she only made humming sounds, and drew caricatures of me.

Hitherto I had always helped her on and off with her coat; now I told her that she was old enough to do this for herself. She would not, however, but held out an arm, repeating, more and more angrily, "Pull, do pull! You've got to pull!"—but I repeated that she must take off her coat by herself. At last I told her that I could only suppose that she wasn't feeling well to-day, and in that case we could not do anything. I busied myself with something else. She was extremely angry, but I let her sit through her hour in her overcoat. I repeated this manœuvre three times. On the last occasion her mother told me that Anne wanted to invite me to her birthday party. The next time she came she again held out her sleeve, looking at me defiantly; I took no notice, and after that she put her coat on and off by herself. When her birthday came round I was unwell and could not go to see her; I wrote to her, and she at once wrote in reply, although she was coming to me on the following day.

Her mother reported further progress; in the school playground she had spoken to other children in a whisper, and in class she had once written on the blackboard. With me too she made further progress; she wrote, read, and played.

In speaking she had now adopted a new tone; she spoke either in a whisper or in a shrill, bird-like little voice.

When her sister had diphtheria she had to stay away for three weeks; at Christmas she came again with fancy-work she had done by herself, and she had even asked her mother if she might work something for me. She was very clever with her hands, and her needlework—like her mother's—was especially fine and exact.

Early in January her visits began again. She still spoke in a whisper or in a bird-like voice, seldom normally. From time to time she was still obstinate. I spoke to her again on the theme 'princess and servant,' and told her that she could not get out of this attitude unless she had a little more courage—enough to venture on a different kind of behaviour.

Next time the mother told me that in school—according to her schoolfellows—during the break she had suddenly sung a few notes aloud (she had not yet sufficient courage to speak).

When she was again obstinate with me I repeated all I had told her, and added that she must surely know that I was very pleased to have her there, but that if she did not wish to she need not come again. On the way home she told her mother, crying, without further explanation, " I can't do anything about it." The result was that for the first time she answered the teacher, softly, in class, and a few days later, in response to a very kindly request, she had read aloud. She continued, of course, to come to me.

It now appeared that her promotion at Easter would depend on her reading something aloud to the headmaster of the school. I had spoken to her about this, telling her that she could do everything at least as well as the other children; now she must have the courage to get right out of her exceptional position, for things would go very badly with her if she was not promoted. At the beginning of February her teacher went with her to the headmaster's room; and then she read aloud to him—though in a very faint voice—and answered some questions.

With me she still spoke softly, and often in a bird-like or twittering voice, but often normally.

Now we began to practise shaking hands; hitherto she had never offered to shake hands with me, neither on arriving nor on leaving. I explained that refusing to take a person's hand meant, " I don't like you! " and since she herself was very anxious that people should like her, she must have some thought for other people. It was again rather difficult for her to get out of an accustomed attitude. She began in this way: putting on her knitted glove, she left one finger of the glove empty, and offered this, half in jest and half seriously, in order to avoid direct contact. We practised this systematically, so that she offered more and more fingers to be taken, until at last the whole hand was offered.

At school she entered more and more into the work of the class, in which she was greatly helped by the fact that she was reckoned the most intelligent child in the class; and out of school she was lively, talkative, and wild. She was promoted at Easter with a good report, which, however, contained the remark that nothing could be said as yet in respect of her success in viva voce examination, since she had only recently begun to speak in class. I called attention to this, with the brief comment, " A pity, because in the next report there are as many marks for that as for the written work."

After Easter her daily visits were discontinued; she then came three times a week and, later on, twice a week. When she went with her mother and sister to her grandmother's during the long vacation she got into touch with the neighbour's children; hesitantly at first, but then she got on very well with them. She also went on little errands. She was still rather shy at first with strangers, but she gradually grew more confident.

Some years have passed since the end of her treatment. I have now known Anne for many years, and she comes to see me several times a year. After leaving school she graduated from the municipal *Handelsschule* (commercial college), where she was among the best pupils, and then obtained a post in an office, in which she gave complete satisfaction. So she had quite abandoned the role of the 'dumb girl.'[2]

Anne was a cossetted child. Owing to her frail constitution and various organic weaknesses (the cause of the spastic troubles could not be ascertained, but at all events she had an excessively labile nervous system, and the alimentary canal showed some inadequacy) she had more difficulty in finding her footing than would a healthy child. The incident of the father's outbursts of anger in respect of nocturnal disturbances so worked upon the child's mind that she

[2] " The clinical picture of the 'dumb girl' reminds us of the condition of schizophrenic mutism, especially as the stereotyped behaviour, the katatonic attitude, the conspicuous negativism with sudden outbreaks of excitement, and the bizarre and childish behaviour, also point in this direction. Only the knowledge of her very different behaviour towards mother and sister and her uninhibited expression in writing encouraged one to assume the existence of a neurotic inhibition and justified therapeutic optimism." (For this notice I should like to thank Dr. Alexandra Adler, Boston, and Dr. Ernst Haase, formerly of Berlin.)

believed herself surrounded by enemies, and therefore clung all the more closely to her mother. The mother, on the other hand, in view of the child's delicate health, thought she could not give her too much care and help; she made everything easy for her, and thereby prevented her from learning by experience that difficulties can be overcome. In this way the child formed the fixed opinion: "All people are bad except my mother, who does everything to serve me." When the child grew older and began to come into contact with people her rule of conduct was already established: "If I can't have things as they are when I'm with mother—if I can't be a princess—I won't have anything to do with people."

Quite as a matter of course, in accordance with her dynamic law (unconsciously, indeed), she excluded everything that would bring her into contact with others: that is, speech, the exchange of glances, handshaking.

Her behaviour during her first days at school showed how discouraged she was. When she saw that she could not enter into the life of the school she had to turn her weakness into strength, and win a special position for herself by her attitude—as she had done in the kindergarten. She did actually obtain the recognition which she needed; the children struggled to sit beside her, and called her 'the dumb girl'; and her teacher was at her service; but she paid a high price for all this. When she came to me for treatment she was able at first to get her way even with me, and to get the upper hand of me, since for weeks and months together I was intensively occupied with her while she employed her depreciatory and asocial tactics against me. However, during this period the mother-child symbiosis was broken down, and a bridge built which led to the community. The intelligent co-operation of the mother, the teacher's patience, and her experiences in the clinic, by which—even though she was still dumb—she most intelligently profited, very slowly enabled her to understand the meaning of her behaviour, of which she had until then been unconscious. Hesitatingly, at first, she ventured gradually to do as others did, and saw that she was not disgracing herself (the greatest dread of a cossetted child), until at last she found the courage for complete normality.

Her aim was, to be an autocrat, and she continued to attain it by the most varied means; by behaving like a child at the breast (as during the consultation in the doctor's clinic), or by adopting the role of the 'dumb girl'; or she got her way through aggression and attempted depreciation (her derisive laughter, her caricatures), or in the posture of the 'princess' she had every one else at her service.

III

A Case of Play-Therapy[1]

HANS, aged 9, the son of very wealthy parents, suffers from intermittent, convulsive, twitching movements of the head, shoulders, and upper part of the body. He constantly scratches himself all over, often until he draws blood. He is given to excessive masturbation.

He is a bad scholar; in particular, he has great difficulty with his spelling. Always inattentive and childish, he is often entirely unable to grasp ideas which are quite familiar to children of 6; so that one might suspect that he was mentally deficient but for the fact that in other respects he gives evidence of good average intelligence. Extremely sensitive, he is rather liable to outbursts of rage, when he rails against the offender in coarse and insulting language, and is quite unable to control himself. In his class (he attends a private school) he is completely isolated; he has no sort of contact with other children.

His mother states that Hans is greatly attached to her; so much so that during the days of her periods his behaviour is especially insufferable, even when mother and child are separated. Hans has the warmest admiration for his father, who holds an important position, and cannot give much thought to the child. And he has a brother, two years his senior, to whom he is greatly attached; according to their mother the two boys " are mutually sufficient; they don't need other children." The mother insists that she and her husband are both difficult people, both isolated and unsociable. So, incidentally, the fact emerges that Hans has an unfortunate inheritance from both sides—from her mother and her husband's father.

Previous history: Hans is the third child of this marriage.

[1] Published in *Int. Zeitschr. für Individualpsychologie,* Vienna, Moritz Perles, 12th year, vol. III.

First, there was a still-born girl child; two years later came Hans's brother, and two years later again, Hans himself. At the time of his birth his mother suffered acute pain, as owing to the position of the child a nerve was subjected to pressure. Parturition was extremely difficult (forceps were used). Hans was a sturdy child, but extremely nervous and restless; from the very first day he was troublesome, crying with alarming persistency. His mother fed him herself. She says that at this time she herself cried a great deal, as she was dreadfully depressed. Even as a suckling the child was given to fits of anger, and masturbated so persistently that nothing could be done about it. On the advice of a specialist he was sent to a children's hospital, where after a period of observation he was to be put into a plaster of paris jacket on account of his masturbation. Hans was ten days in the hospital without any outbursts of rage; the first fit of anger occurred when his mother came to see him. He was then put into plaster of paris, but only for a little while, since there was an outbreak of an infectious illness in the hospital and he had to be sent home.

Hans learnt to speak and to walk in a fairly normal manner, but until his seventh year he wetted his bed. Of childish maladies he contracted measles and whooping-cough. At a very early age he suffered from extreme sensitiveness of the skin. Exactly when the jerky movements and the scratching first began his mother was unable to say; at all events, they had been troubling him for years. The doctors advised the mother to keep the nervous child as much as possible in the open air. Accordingly his father bought a country house within easy reach of the city, and there, during the first years of his life, he spent the spring, summer, and autumn. His mother was constantly with him.

This country life did the child good, and he became rather less restless. In the winter he often travelled with his parents, but the bed-wetting did not stop until his admission to a sleeping-car—he was then 7—was made conditional upon his cleanliness.

Since Hans was not to be exposed to the strain of going to school a tutor was engaged for him; but he was so infatuated with the boy that Hans learnt absolutely nothing from him. Eighteen months later his parents sent him to the above-mentioned private school; but there were such gaps in his education that he had at first to be given private lessons.

At the beginning of his treatment he had been at this private school for eighteen months. His whole condition was then so bad that remedial treatment was a sheer necessity.

The foregoing data were generally confirmed during a consultation with his father. But the father—unlike the mother—does not consider that it is good for the two brothers to be always together to the exclusion of other company; he would prefer that the children should mix with others of their own age, for the elder brother, who attends a grammar school and is a good scholar, is quite isolated in his class.

A conversation with Hans's schoolmistress confirmed the fact that in respect of his work, and also his general behaviour, he was out of his place in the class.

With the permission of the parents, a consultation was held with the family doctor, who had known Hans since birth. No fresh conclusions were arrived at. The doctor laid even greater stress on the inherited taint. One could not really expect any results from therapeutic treatment, since in this case the constitutional factor must be taken into account. " Hans is simply a psychopath—a bad case." Despite this by no means encouraging prognosis, I decided to make an experiment. As an alleged friend of their mother, I visited the house in order to become acquainted with the children.

Hans is a sturdy-looking, well-developed youngster, with fine, expressive eyes, in contrast with his coarse mouth. He is terribly restless, constantly twitching and scratching himself. His facial expression is constantly changing; at one moment it is amiable and apparently interested; and the next moment it is drowsy, indifferent, unamiable. His superficial manners are impeccable; he is pleasant and attentive to a guest, and offers to show the latter his playroom.

The household is run on a generous scale; and the playroom—which is more like a drill-hall in its proportions—is filled with everything a juvenile heart could desire: electrical apparatus, toy railways, motor-cars, games, and books. One thing is clear—these children can really have nothing more to wish for.

We speak of the school; he likes going to school; his favourite subject is drawing, and he shows me sketches that reveal a strong feeling for colour. " I'm worst of all in grammar! "—Hans's brother was about to leave the room, but now he turns round and dances one step back into the room, saying, " I have the best marks in grammar! " Hans blushes a fiery red and is plainly annoyed. The situation is as clear as though a searchlight were turned upon it; Hans, the second child, the younger brother, is struggling to keep up with the older brother, and feels that he is pushed aside by him, for he is a good scholar.

After this first visit I explained to the boy's mother how matters stood, and begged her as far as possible to avoid situations which might confirm Hans in his opinion. I emphasized the fact that the individual-psychological treatment does not consist in removing difficulties, but that nevertheless it is often necessary, especially at the beginning of a treatment, to avoid needless friction; to observe, as it were, a sort of close season. It is natural that the mother did not find it very easy to regard the relation between the two brothers in this completely new light. Still, it was clear to me that I should do best—contrary to my usual practice—to undertake the treatment of *this* child only inside his environment. Under the pretext that I was writing a book about children, so that Hans could help me by describing his experiences with children, I was able to visit the house frequently.

Hans had made preparations for my next visit, having

arranged a number of picture postcards and circulars which he wanted to show me. He was now very confidential. When I was ready to leave he accompanied me. Just as we were leaving the house, a few children came towards us, among whom was a boy in Hans's class, who at once called out, " Here's the lousy beggar! " (Hans had apparently earned this nickname by his frequent scratching.) In a blind rage Hans fell upon the boy, and I had some difficulty in separating the two fighting-cocks. We continued on our way, but it was not easy to quiet him, and he spoke excitedly and contemptuously of the other boy: " No one in the class likes him." In response to my inquiries, he told me that at first he had not been able to make friends with any of the children, but now he had a girl friend, and was getting on very well with the other children. (This was contradicted by the statements of the adults.) After this I told him about a little girl who had always been with her mother, and who could not make friends when she went to school, because she was not used to doing so, and would not venture to mix with other children. Hans, to all seeming quite uninterested, played with his little walking-stick. He had quite confidingly taken my arm, but he kept on withdrawing his hand in order to scratch himself. To my question, " Have you any pain there? " he replied, " No, it itches! " And to my further inquiry, " Have you anything the matter with your skin—a little blister or anything? " he replied, rather vehemently, " No, there's nothing, nothing at all, I've never had anything like that! " This excited answer shows very plainly how sensitive the boy is, so that he feels the very suggestion that he might have some uncleanly affection of the skin as humiliating to his sense of personality.

On my next visit I found his mother in a state of great excitement. " It's the first time the boy has told a lie; he took some chocolate, and he lied about it! " I explained that this behaviour was only to be regarded as further evidence that the child feels himself to be wronged and is extremely unsure of himself. Presently the mother told me:

" Hans wants to go on strike; he has told enough now, and it's his brother's turn! " (There was here a touch of girlish jealousy, by which Hans was trying to influence me, but we soon got over that.)

In the following period I had several conversations with the mother, who had to be won over to the individual-psychological way of regarding things; she found it very difficult to believe that Hans was always feeling that he was being slighted. Christmas came. After the holidays the mother told me that Hans had been behaving better, which she attributed to his delight in his Christmas presents. (It was probably largely due also to the fact that the great nervous tension which going to school always entailed for Hans was relaxed during this period.) On my first visit after the holidays I noted a much more positive attitude in the boy. He greeted me with the statement that " he had a treat for me to-day "; he was going to tell me about a dream.

I had often asked him if he had any dreams which would be of assistance in respect of the book I was writing, but hitherto he had never been able to tell me anything. It seemed that this dream of his was a waking dream, and since he informed me that it was very long I asked him to dictate it to me.

Hans's attitude during this dictation was interesting; he walked up and down the room with his hands behind his back, frowning portentously. But secretly he felt so delighted that from time to time he broke out into derisive laughter, especially when I asked him to dictate less rapidly, as I could not keep up with him. He gave a perfect imitation of his father—of the General Director dictating to his shorthand-typist. And here follows the dream, which I recorded verbatim (except in places where Hans, in childish fashion, continued his narrative with an " and then "; also a few full stops are inserted):

" When we were in Hiddensöe and my father and brother had already left I swam some way out into the sea with my mother."

(The family had actually been to Hiddensöe; but it is not a fact that the father and brother were the first to leave. So Hans created the situation he needed: to be alone with his mother.) " But I wasn't yet able to swim properly . . ." (The mother really ought to have known this: there is no relying on her. But her punishment follows quickly.)

" . . . and I was drowned. My mother swam back directly, waited a few days, and was very sad. As I wasn't found she went back to B—. They were all very sad at home, they cried a lot and wore mourning." (The confirmation of his value.)

" . . . Only my brother wouldn't do that."

(Here is an unmistakable expression of Hans's attitude toward his brother.)

" After a few days a man came and said: ' I should like to have the summer overcoat, the pocket-book, the watch and the fountain-pen of your dead son.' "

(He possesses these articles; they are of the finest quality; and it gives him pleasure to enumerate them.)

" But I was alive again in the sea, quite grown-up and very rich."

(The impossible becomes possible; intermediate stages are taken at a jump; one perceives the neurotic ambition. It is a curious thing that with this child, who lives in luxury, wealth should play so great a part. Hans very often says that he wants to be rich, to make money; which is perhaps intelligible only if one realizes that this child always has the feeling that he is being slighted or deprived, and that wealth and money signify the means of exerting power.)

" I went off to B—and came to the railway station and drove home in a big Mercedès."

(Hans takes a great interest in motor-cars and knows all the makes.)

" My mother and brother were just playing ' Policeman and motor-car '; my father was making a business call."

(The faithless mother is playing ' Policeman and motor-car '—Hans's favourite game—with his brother, whom Hans depreciates by leaving him a little boy, playing a childish game, while he, Hans, returns home as a grown-up person.)

" God had told every one I know that I had grown up, but not that I was coming back, and now I arrived unexpectedly."

(He is so important that God Himself takes an interest in his affairs, but he is also so clever that he outwits God.)

" My mother and my brother embraced me and were overjoyed. Then my father came in, and he was enraptured; and our maid, too, was very glad."

(It gives him such pleasure to think how beloved he is that he cannot exclude even his brother.)

" My brother had been making something or other electrical; I gave him a lighthouse and a circle of light round the lighthouse."

(Hans is now quite ' on top '; he not only gives presents to his brother, he even radiates light!)

" After a few days I said, in the evening, ' Now I will give my brother his postponed Christmas present.' "

(What he has given him hitherto is not enough; he loads his brother with presents.)

" We went into the house next door, a perfectly empty house, where there was a great square hall. There were electric trains there, landscapes, villages, towns and countries: Europe, Asia, Australia, America and Africa."

(No more and no less than on the entire globe!)

" If one turned a lever to the right everything worked automatically; otherwise everything had to be set in motion by other levers and press-buttons. I gave all that to my brother! "

(So far Hans was only tall, grown-up, rich—and therefore powerful; but now he made his brother a present of the whole world, which could be set going by pressing a switch; he was now all-powerful, god-like!)

" Another evening I said, 'Now for the present for my parents and my brother.' We got into my Mercedès and drove to Hamburg."

(He had often made this journey by motor car; it is interesting to note that the car is *his* Mercedès.)

" When we came to Hamburg we got into a little motor-boat and went to a tiny island, where there was a gigantic motor-boat of mine."

(How he gets his effects by contrast! Of course, *he* has a gigantic motor-boat! Perhaps later on this boy might do something in the artistic or possibly the dramatic line.)

" We went for a long way in this. Downstairs was a long gangway with doors on both sides. One led into a little room in which there were two white rabbits with blue spots and red eyes."

(He is particularly fond of rabbits, but here they are fairy creatures.)

" In this room, too, there was my bed. When I fell asleep they always climbed up around me, because they were so fond of me, and I of them."

(Here we see the child's need of love and tenderness; even when he is asleep he must be loved, if only by the silly little rabbits.)

" On the other side of the gangway was another door; there was a big room in which there was a miniature electric railway. I was on the bridge all day steering the ship, talking to another man who was always there. So we sailed to America! "

(In a final apotheosis we see the boy as leader, steering the ship toward a new world, but still capable of amusing himself and conversing.)

It was very tempting to make Hans realize, by means of this waking fantasy, his mistaken attitude to life and his monstrously exaggerated ambition. But as I did not know whether he was yet ready to accept and ponder such explanations, I preferred to go to work with caution.

Hans was still positive in his attitude. He rummaged

among his playthings to find something that would very well serve our purpose: namely, 'the village'; little houses, town hall, post office, school house, hotel, etc. with trees and gardens. As he also possessed a mountain railway, he began to lay out the village on the floor of the playroom, and then to build a road from the village to the mountain railway. In all this he showed himself to be extremely dexterous, as he is always when using his hands. To a pertinent question of mine, "Wouldn't you like to be an architect?" he replied, "No, one can't make enough money by that." Again, money and the longing for wealth.

We now began to bring people (figures) into the game. A railroad connexion was made from the distant town to the village, and a motor bus service ran to the mountain railway, etc. Finally, with the help of the figures, two families were founded in the town, each with two children, a boy and a girl, all on friendly terms. In the game Hans now saw his own problem as in a looking-glass. One boy, Werner (who resembled Hans) had difficulties at home (in respect of his sister, whom he considered was preferred before himself); at school (in respect of other children, and his work). Now conversations took place—initiated by myself—which, on the one hand, exhibited Werner-Hans in his erroneous mode of behaviour, while on the other hand his friend Paul (the son of the other family) gave psychological explanations. Hans has a great liking for noisy games; he makes the locomotives whistle, the motor-buses and electric trains rush along; he builds garages in his village, and his greatest delight is to make his big fleet of motor-cars set off with a great uproar. More and more things are woven into the game. While at first Hans left the initiative entirely to me, he gradually became more active; school excursions and feasts were organized (plenty of toys were available), and everything that related to Hans was debated: his conduct at home, the conflict between the brothers, his attitude in the community of the school, his unsociableness, etc. Werner is naturally a poor scholar, who has no self-confidence, and is bad at spelling. To the question, why Werner is always allowed to use such bad language, Hans replied, "He regards himself as a grown-up person!"

This playing at real life is beginning to have a good effect. Hans is becoming quieter; the teacher gives a better report of him; the scratching and the jerky movements are much reduced when he is concentrated on the game. A dispute with the maidservant, which I happened to witness, was not followed by any outburst of anger; Hans behaved reasonably, and the matter was quickly forgotten. In a conversation with his mother the latter told me that there was a notable improvement, but she complained that the boy still harboured animosity towards his brother (which formerly she had refused to admit). As an example, she described a recent incident at table, when Hans had behaved very badly to his brother. Hans finds it intolerable that three times a week the family speaks French at table, a Frenchwoman being present; his brother is able to join in the conversation, while he is told, commiseratingly: "If *you* will learn French you will be able to understand what we say." One can sympathize with him. But generally speaking Hans is improving in various ways; he is much less irritable, enters much more readily into the work of the school, according to his teacher, and has already begun to associate with the other children. I had occasion to note his increased perseverance recently, when I found him occupied with a very complicated jigsaw puzzle; he spent an hour and a half over it, and went on until he had put the whole thing together. During this time there were no restless movements, and he did not scratch himself. On being questioned, his mother told me that during her last period she had, for the first time, no trouble with Hans.

A slight middle-ear inflammation kept Hans in bed for some days. When he got up again he was more restless than he had been of late. A few days later, when he had worked off his energies in games, he was normal again. The doctor wants him to have a change of air, and it has been suggested that his mother should take him to a winter sports centre. At school he is doing quite well again, and although it is perhaps a pity, now that he is doing so well, to take him away again, his physical condition necessitates a holiday. When he leaves home his treatment will be concluded; it has lasted twelve weeks in all.

At last Hans has been told of the intended journey. On my next visit he tells me how delighted he is: "But unfortunately it's only a fortnight." I profess my surprise at this remark; he ought to consider how privileged he is in comparison with other children—his brother, for example, who would certainly have liked to go with him. The word 'privileged' had hardly been spoken when something quite unexpected happened. Hans threw himself on to the sofa, struck out with his hands and feet, and shrieked, in the greatest excitement: "I don't want to hear that word, I don't want to hear that word!" When I asked him, in astonishment, what on earth was the matter, he continued, crying, "I know very well you mean it's like it is with Werner!" He was alluding to our game—and showing that he had already understood the serious element in the game.

By adducing examples, I made it clear to him that one uses this word when one wishes to indicate that one person is more fortunate than another. At this he cooled off, and said, finally, "I know now how you mean it, but I don't like the word."

I now come to my last visit before his trip. We again spoke of his approaching holiday, and I said, casually, "Yes, travel is one of the finest things in life," to which he replied, very seriously, "No, that's not right. The finest thing in life is good health and love; compared with them riches aren't worth a thing!" This opposition of love and wealth seemed to me very opportune. We discussed the matter, saying that a person who loves and gives his love to a number of people is always growing richer, while a person who is closely attached to *one* other person is stultifying himself—as when a child is attached only to his father. To this Hans responded, thoughtfully, " But it can be the mother; you told me once about a little girl who couldn't make friends with any one." So when he had been playing in the sand with his walking-stick, apparently quite uninterested (during our walk together after my first visit) he had been listening carefully, and had accepted what was intended for him.

I now had to approve of the playthings which Hans wanted to take with him. Between certain comical objects of which he was especially fond—a rabbit and a ' Mr. and Mrs. Clown '—he could not make up his mind. To my suggestion that if he didn't want to be bothered with them perhaps other children would take pleasure in them, he replied, with embarrassment, " Oh, I don't know yet whether I shall play with other children."

This gave me an opportunity of saying that every child ought to like playing with other children, but that a good many children have so little self-confidence that they don't show that they would like to play. The child who has the greatest courage takes the first step! Silently Hans put the toys with the things he was taking with him.

On bidding me good-bye he said, " Of course, we shall see each other again. That is, one can never say ' of course,' because one might die. But why imagine such ugly things! " Here we see the old line of thought: the child with the hesitant attitude: one must have a care, one can never know what misfortune is threatening! Yet there was an improvement: pessimism must be overcome!

Hans was away for about six weeks. His health benefited greatly; he behaved very nicely during the journey, and got on capitally with other children.

A post-card written during the journey reveals his mood. I should have mentioned that last time we said good-bye we agreed to communicate with each other in doggerel verse, which he thought great fun. And now he wrote, " I've a lot to tell you for your book when I return. *Viel Schnee und viel Sonne, wenig Weh und viel Wonne, hat Hans.*" (More or less: " Lots of snow and lots of sun, little trouble and lots of fun.")

He came back after having had a very good time. At school he did well in every way; the physical symptoms—the twitching movements, the scratching, the masturbation—had disappeared. Shortly after his return he developed a serious affection of the kidneys. He had to leave school at once, as he needed the greatest care, special diet, and medical treatment. There was reason to fear that all that had been achieved with such pains would now be lost. Happily this was not the case, although there were no further consultations. After an absence of some months Hans went back to school, cured; he entered into the work of his class and got on well with the other children. At Easter he went up to the grammar school, and a year later he was promoted straightway to the next form. Further inquiry elicited the fact that he had settled down and found his place in the little community of his class.

Hans is the typical spoilt or cossetted child, who in consequence of various organic weaknesses (labile nervous system, sensitive skin, sensitive urinary apparatus) is handicapped as against a healthy child. The boy confronted life without confidence. In consequence of harmful environmental influences (the nervous mother, his parents' unfortunate ideas, a certain amount of repression exerted by his elder brother, and the over-indulgence with which he was treated, which was aggravated by wealth) the boy acquired an oppressive sense of inferiority. This resulted in an exaggerated striving for recognition and limitless ambition, from which arose his dynamic law: to excel his father, who had hitherto been for him the embodiment of superiority, and to be like God Himself (who gives the world away and sets it in motion by pressing a switch). His aim, therefore, is to achieve the greatest possible power! Hans is a fighter! His weapons are aggressiveness, intolerance (active), inability to learn and to take one's place with others (apparently passive). The addition of physical symptoms is a means of drawing attention to himself.

Hans declared that " the finest thing in life is good health and love, wealth is worth nothing in comparison! " In the language of individual-psychology, this would mean: The finest thing in life is the capacity for healthy, active co-operation within the community and for the community! And here Hans really confessed his adherence to the doctrine of individual-psychology, which sets itself the problem of transforming the " discouraged victim of ambition " (Adler) into a courageous member of the community.

IV

"I can't get up in the morning"

"I HAVE come on account of a trouble which isn't really anything at all; I can't get up early, I can't get out of bed punctually," complained a young man of 23, whom we will call Paul.

Paul, who has a twin brother, fills an important post, notwithstanding his youth. He is technical director in a business founded by his uncle, which has developed into a firm of international standing. His brother is employed in the same business. And now Paul describes what happens every morning: He is wakened early, he wants to get up, but he doesn't find it possible. Then his brother appears, and reminds him of the time, but it is no use. Paul tells himself that after all he needn't really be at the office so early, since he has reliable subordinates, and then, when at last he really does mean to get up, he falls into a sort of half-sleep, in which he tries to solve his current problems—mostly of a technical nature. In this way he reaches the office every day an hour or two hours later than he ought. It isn't that he is shirking his work; he is a fanatic for work, and he generally goes on working for hours after the others have finished; so that he does his work properly, and although he has conscientious scruples, as far as that goes it really doesn't matter if he is late in the morning. But the thing may soon have unpleasant and even disastrous results. He has now got to undertake a new job of work; he will have to go abroad and inspect the firm's factories in other countries. And he is feeling terribly worried; he is supposed to look after the technical side of the business, and he is always unpunctual; what is going to happen? Asked if he manages to get up in time when he has to go on a journey or is making an excursion (he had just been speaking of a ski-running excursion) he replies that he has no difficulty in getting up, but for hours afterwards he suffers from headache and depression.

Concerning his early childhood, Paul tells me that at birth he was the weaker of the pair of twins, and during the first eighteen months of his life he was very ill, so that his mother had to give him special care and attention. Towards the second year there was a change; he grew stronger and outstripped his brother, who from that time onwards was smaller and weaker, and needed greater care. His mother tells him that from this point he gave her a great deal of trouble by his bad behaviour; he was headstrong, and always wanted to be the centre of attention, which had not been the case earlier (simply because he had then been his mother's chief anxiety). His mother, who formerly had always been very tender and affectionate, was now often very angry, and even struck him sometimes. His father played no particular part in his life.

Asked if he could remember some incident of his early childhood, Paul said that when he was five years old he went with his mother to visit some relations abroad. They lived in a villa; there were no other children, and no one paid much attention to him, so he set to work and smashed everything he could. The adult Paul relates this incident with a comfortable smile; even to-day he enjoys the sense of superiority which he experienced as a child. As a matter of fact, the incident shows that he was a child who liked to do things that annoyed people, and who protested whenever he found himself in a situation which did not altogether please him. He encountered no difficulties at school; he was a very intelligent boy, made good progress, and was on terms of friendship with his masters. But then there was a change; he had masters whom he did not like, and he simply did not co-operate with them, although he worked particularly well under the masters whom he liked. This, of course, did not pay in the long run, so that he fell behind, and for the last two years at school he had to have private lessons from a coach in order to matriculate at the proper time. The uncle in whose business he was employed had played a great part in his life from early childhood; he was the brother of Paul's mother, and filled a decisive role in the family. So Paul had learnt very early in life that one must be clever, industrious, and influential, and then one is regarded as a little god.

After matriculating he entered his uncle's business, and in a comparatively short time he had achieved a considerable position. Concerning his relations with other people, Paul asserts that he has always had friends who think highly of him. He must add, however, that he is still on friendly terms with two men who are definitely his superior; they are older than he, and in the city (a capital city of medium size) they are regarded as persons of exceptional ability. Where women are concerned he always takes the initiative; he has nothing to do with women who are not submissive; if later on he were to think of marriage he would perhaps want a wife who would be a real comrade.

If we now draw a comprehensive portrait, we shall find that we are dealing with a delicate, cossetted child, who grew out of his weakness and acquired a strongly emphasized self-esteem; so strongly emphasized that he was evidently in danger of doubting his own importance. In the behaviour of the child, in the naughtiness of which his mother complained, in the acts of protest during a visit to relatives (which he remembered and described), we see the child's efforts to draw attention to himself. The slackness at school when he no longer liked his masters shows that this was a child who would co-operate only so long as it pleased him to do so, and who did not readily submit to dictation. Already one can perceive the structure of his dynamic law, which proclaims "*My* will be done!" His aim is always to be 'on top.' This appears later in his relations with his fellows. And even where it is not apparent, as in his relations with his two older friends, he is conscious of an enhancement of his sense of personality, because they are men for whom the whole city has a special regard. We see the same thing in his relation with women, though here, when he thinks of an eventual marriage, the doubt emerges as to whether his attitude is what it should be.

His inability to get up in the morning is a protest against allowing himself to be dictated to, even by a generally accepted rule, which declares that one should rest at certain times and go to work at certain times. *He* works when other people are resting. Even the depression and the headache when special circumstances compel him to rise early show that here an attack has been made on his most sacred possession—his independence. From his earliest childhood his uncle has been his ideal: the omnipotent uncle who has so many people under his command: him he endeavours to imitate; he must assert his will, he must be recognized as a person of exceptional importance. In this urge toward exaggerated self-assertion he can only associate with people in respect of whom he is ' on top '; he protests against the requirements of the community, for even his inability to get up in the morning is a sign that he has not the ' team spirit.' And this he can hardly explain to himself, for he could not be ' on top ' if he had to make this confession. So he has to make excuses (unconsciously, of course), saying that it isn't really so necessary to get up early; or he has to attempt to solve his technical problems while half asleep; which again amounts to an excuse. Hitherto Paul has enjoyed very favourable circumstances, and has always tried to take the easiest way; the difficulties arise when this no longer seems available.

Paul quite understood these explanations, and—although they were not very gratifying—considered that they seemed very largely correct. He came to see me once more, merely to tell me that our recent conversations had done him good; that he was now rising punctually and was not accepting any excuses. In further confirmation he sent me a postcard written during one of his journeys; he was getting on well and " rising in the morning like a young god! "

V

Two Anxiety-Neuroses

(1)

A YOUNG woman of 24, pale, with dark shadows under her eyes, and very restless in her manner, complains of severe cardiac and digestive troubles. She is studying music, and cannot work, as she is unable to concentrate. She has fits of anxiety, especially when she thinks of the examination for which she will have to sit in eighteen months' time.

A medical examination reveals spastic vascular obstructions. The patient might be described as of the Bassedowoid type; her troubles, to judge from the results of the examination, appear to be somewhat exaggerated.

Previous history. The patient knows nothing about her parents. Before she was six months old she was adopted by a childless widow. Her present mother, a refined, cultivated woman, the widow of a Geheimrat, who was no longer young when she adopted the child, was then living with her own aged mother.

She looked after the child herself to a great extent, and she also employed a nursery governess, so that the patient was brought up by three women, who spoiled and petted her, all the more because she was an exceptionally pretty child. In her very early childhood she suffered from whooping-cough and middle ear inflammation; she caught cold very easily, and those in charge of her anxiously tried to guard her against undue exposure. She did not remain long in the kindergarten, as she did not like it, and apart from this she hardly ever saw anything of other children. At the age of 6 she was sent to school; that is, she attended a small private class. At first she got on very well, because her governess was always with her; then she found the work difficult, especially arithmetic; in her second year at school she had such difficulty in keeping up with the others that she was taken away and given private lessons for six months.

After this she went to another private school. She was a model child as regards behaviour, but found the work very difficult. At home she never did her homework alone; if she could not do it she cried, or turned obstinate. Once when she was reprimanded at school she cried until her bad mark was cancelled. With one of her kindergarten teachers she tried to get her way by amiability and affection; with another, who did not impress her particularly, by aggressiveness. She was twelve years old when she first struck a match; before that she had always been afraid to do so. In every connexion, anxiety played a great part all through her childhood; she would not sleep in the dark, the door had to be left open, etc. She had no friends during her schooldays. At the age of sixteen she concluded her not very successful scholastic career. In order to learn housekeeping she was sent for six months to a boarding-house on the Baltic coast, but she did not work very hard there. Then she came home again, and for a year she attended a finishing school, but she did not like it. After this she obtained a commercial post in a large export business, whose director-in-chief was a personal friend of the family. She admits that she was there on an exceptional footing; everything was made easy for her, and she was treated as a favoured employee. But when something happened that displeased her she resigned her position. She now thought of taking up gymnastics; before the final entrance examination there was a three months' preparatory course at the seaside. At first she found this 'great fun'; but when the leader, about a month before the end of the course, spoke rather more definitely about the coming entrance examination she had a serious heart attack, and had to give up her gymnastic training immediately. Various doctors were consulted, and various diagnoses were made; weakness of the cardiac muscles, cardiac neurosis, etc. So a year went by, spent partly at home and partly in travelling; and all the time she was tended and petted by her anxious mother. But at last she was again confronted by the problem of her future vocation. And now she began to study music, but here again, after about a year, 'it was no longer amusing.' As we have seen, she was finding the work very difficult, and the thought of the examination filled her with anxiety.

RECOLLECTIONS OF CHILDHOOD

From her second year. She was lying in her little bed, drinking by the hour from her bottle. Her mother was sitting by her, and had apparently been 'giving her a good talking to,' and she was thinking 'not just now.'

Listening to this, we can understand that she has never, as she tells me, been a hearty eater, and that she suffers from digestive troubles.

From her first years at school. When, on account of some misdemeanour, she had been punished by being deprived of her supper—a slice of a big fancy cake—she glanced out of the window while the others were eating and spoke of the green buds on the chestnut trees. Thereupon she poured a glass of wine over the rest of the cake.

Another recollection of this period. She was punished for some offence by having her doll taken away for a few days. When it was returned she had a long conversation with the doll, saying that she supposed it must have been away from home; what sort of a time had it had, and did it rain, etc.?

Another recollection of her schooldays. If she couldn't do anything she would duck down behind the back of the child in front of her.

All her recollections are agreed in revealing her dread of failure. The first, in particular, reveals defiance, and her intense striving for superiority, which compels her to draw a veil over negative experiences and to distort the reality if she finds it displeasing; at the same time vigorous aggression reveals itself.

In the course of the first consultation the patient spoke of some young cousins for whom she had a great respect, but on whom, apparently, she made no great impression. She is greatly interested in the other sex, and she tells me how she looks for adventure when she is making a journey. When she had to wait for some hours at a railway station she went for a drive in the forest with a strange man, and took to her heels when he became importunate. Six months ago, at a ball, she made the acquaintance of a young man, with whom she got on very well; they met again afterwards, and finally they became engaged, though she did not tell her mother anything about it. This young man is of no particular family; he is a petty official; socially he is beneath her, but they understand each other, and this is the first time she has felt this about a man. At last she told her mother of the engagement. Her mother does not approve of it, as the man comes from quite a different environment. She has to admit that she always used to think she would marry a well-to-do man of her own set, who would hold an important position; as for externals, she does not consider that her fiancé is handsome. The question arises: why did she become engaged?

Despite her understanding for her mother's attitude the patient seizes the opportunity of sharply criticizing the latter. Her mother allows her no liberty; she loves her daughter so that she wants always to have her to herself. The daughter does not feel that she can respond with an equally passionate affection, and this often troubles her. Further, her mother is afraid that she works too hard during the term, so that she often doesn't know what she ought to do. It is not a difficult matter to show the patient the whole tenor of her life hitherto in relation to what she has confessed: how she makes a beginning with everything, and then, 'when it is no longer amusing,' drops it immediately; how she is always trying to escape—which is obvious from her reminiscences. She tries by every means to 'get on top': by amiability, affection, aggressiveness, shuffling out of obligations, illness.

She professes to be convinced of the correctness of these explanations, but she also says that things are going better with her now in every way. But it is easy to see that she is pretending, in order to avoid any discussion of her less pleasing points. For this reason the consultations are discontinued, in spite of her protest.

Three months later she appears again, professing that " it has occurred to her " that it was right to discontinue the consultations; now she wants to begin again, with the firm resolve that she won't shuffle out of anything!

The same subjects are discussed; she has really no intimate contact with her mother, and her heart is not in her work; she has few relations with other people, and has never had a friend of her own sex. Her engagement seems to be mainly a sexual relation; she has sometimes very strong sexual impulses.

And finally she confesses—she is looking very ill—that her sexual intercourse with her fiancé is so exhausting that she has fits of crying for hours afterwards. She takes the advice given her—to discuss the matter frankly with her fiancé—but retails everything that has been discussed during her visits to me as her own ideas. She has definitely the upper hand over him; she is always speaking of his inhibitions, which show themselves even in sexual intercourse, and she thinks that if these matters were not satisfactorily adjusted when she was married she would simply run away.

The difficulties which she first alleged as the chief reasons for her visits—such as the inability to concentrate on her work—were very easy to see through. While playing the piano she suddenly thinks of a young man at the training college, and she cannot get him out of her head. Or, when she is working at a theoretical subject, she suddenly becomes afraid that she will not be able to get through the work still to be done before the examination. All these escapist manœuvres are unmasked and shown to be deliberate plans; for example, her fiancé has been speaking to her, proposing —since as regards his relations with her mother the situation is decidedly uncomfortable—that she should marry him as soon as she has sat for her examination; so in good time she takes steps to ensure that the marriage shall not take place just yet. She accepts these explanations, and now she really begins to work at essential subjects, so that in a comparatively short time she has made gratifying progress. She now tells her mother of her sexual relations with her fiancé; not, of course, without unconscious intention, for her fiancé is pressing her more and more urgently to marry him, and she unconsciously hopes that her confession will be a great shock to her mother, who is still wholly influenced by the views of the previous generation, and will perhaps evoke her serious opposition to the match.

And now, one day, the mother comes to me for a consultation. Although she is opposed to the marriage on the grounds already stated, it is comparatively easy to persuade her to adopt a more objective attitude; she even admits that the fiancé is an estimable young man, and she will agree to the marriage, as her daughter thinks that she could not be happy with any one else. The effect of the mother's decision on the patient is that the latter declares, on her next visit, that she certainly wants to get married, but she finds that her fiancé still has too many inhibitions. And as we then go on to discuss her own overbearing manner, which is again utilized as an expedient, she reverts to the familiar locution; the truth has 'dawned upon her'; now everything is clear to her.

Then she falls ill once more; she has an inflamed throat, and heart attacks, which are attributed to the exophthalmic diathesis; for a long while she is unable to attend the college. Her anxious mother, fearing lest her daughter, despite her diligence, might be unable to make up for time lost, advises her to put off sitting for the examination until the following year; to which the patient agrees. Her fiancé, however, wants the marriage to be soon; to which the patient makes the objection that her mother wants her to pass the examination first. And so the three factors—

mother, examination, marriage—are constantly shuffled to and fro in accordance with the patient's need at the moment.

After an initial period without any dreams the patient now brings a number of dreams, of which only one will be cited here: verbatim, as it was written down.

"I am by a big lake; there are chestnut trees growing on the shore; not very tall. There are lots of women, girls, and children there, most of the little ones in perambulators. I can see numbers of perambulators. I collect a lot of chestnuts, only fine ones; this amuses me; I shall make them into little baskets for the children. I have pushed my doll's perambulator a little way into the water; there is a very big doll in it, with long hair; it is greatly admired. I speak now and then, amiably, to people who speak to me, but otherwise I keep myself to myself. It begins to rain, and I say: we shall have to go indoors. The chestnuts must have only a certain definite shape. I take only perfectly smooth, round, glossy, dark-brown nuts, without any scratches; I refuse the others, which are offered me by other young women. I tell them they can keep those for themselves; they are not good enough for me. I am not quite sure whether I am still a child with a pigtail, or a grown-up girl, or a woman. To judge by my behaviour and the doll's perambulator I am a child; I have a pigtail and I feel its weight behind me. On the other hand I seem to myself to be much cleverer, better and wiser than the other women, and also very experienced (womanhood is blended with childhood [pigtail] and childishness [the doll's perambulator and collecting chestnuts]). I consider the matter and ask which side of the chestnuts I ought to have uppermost, the smooth or the dull. The others think this unimportant, frivolous, not worth thinking about, a waste of time. I think it very important; everything in life is important, big things and little. If one doesn't make a beginning with the insignificant things one isn't scrupulous enough about the big important things. I think I am much smaller than in reality; I am even crawling about in the sand and among the fallen leaves, which are damp. I think there's a little dog there too, and I don't seem to myself much bigger than he. We look for chestnuts together; that is, he keeps on running after me; a terrier. The women are sitting on a box of sand, knitting stockings; most of them are looking at me; in any case they are all interested in me, and look up to me. They are working-class women between twenty and forty years of age, and they are all wearing aprons. They are rather lively, all shouting and chattering together, and laughing a great deal. I am the only person running about; the others are sitting still. When I look for chestnuts and rustle the leaves the women sit facing me, and when I am standing by the water they all turn round. I am the principal person. I don't give any orders or express any wishes, but they are all gathered about me in silent respect, although I hold myself rather aloof from them and never mix with the other people. But I have no need to. Although I am still a child I am *much more important* than all the others. Of course, they are only uneducated women; not a single one of them is of my class! They have not, of course, my general culture, so I can boss them a little."

Very striking in this dream is the intense egoism (almost every sentence begins with ' I ') and the crude form in which the antithesis, sense of inferiority and striving for recognition, is expressed. The girl feels little and childish and compares herself with a little dog; on the other hand she seems to herself cleverer, better, and wiser than the others. In a didactic tone, such as she adopts in addressing her lover, she speaks of what is important in life, while she basks in the belief that all the people are interested only in her, and listen to her in silent respect. The rule that the chestnuts must have a certain definite shape shows the peremptory temper of the neurotic requirement. As the centre of general attention, conscious of being *much more important* than the others, she grapples with the social problem, which is forcing itself upon her attention owing to her coming marriage with a man who is not her social equal, and she comes to the conclusion that she can ‘ boss ’ people a little who are not of her own class, and have not the same general culture. The dream shows, too, that in spite of the fact that so many things have ‘ dawned on her,’ she is still very far from being on the right track.

Her mother, and indeed all her relations, say that her fiancé is very greatly improved, which the patient has to admit. She is now beginning to work again, but takes advantage of her fiancé's temporary absence to engage in a very unrestrained flirtation with a fellow-student; which she confesses to her lover on his return. Is this due to her love of truth, or to her repenting of her divagation? It seems that there must be rather different ways of judging such behaviour, for when both the young people—she and her lover—appeared together for a consultation, she was as defiant as a naughty child, while he very quietly insisted that he had the right to demand that such things should not happen. When I expressed the opinion that the incident might be taken as a clear proof that the relation between these two people was not on a proper basis, the patient quickly agreed, which was proof that she was interested in persuading him of the fact, and therefore, that he should not be in too great a hurry to get married.

One day before the summer holidays she comes to me again; things are not well with her; at the beginning of August she is supposed to play a prelude, a sort of preliminary test, and she is very anxious about it, because once more she cannot practice properly. And actually, while playing through the programme on which she has been working for months, the thought suddenly occurs to her: “ What would happen if now you were to strike the wrong note? ” Again it is explained to her that she has found another means of making difficulties for herself and running away from them. She must know by now whether she really wants to pass the examination or not; she can make her way with the teaching diploma which she will certainly obtain, and then she can get married. Very hesitatingly she makes the objection: " I don't know; I don't want to marry at all; sometimes I think I love my fiancé, but then I think I haven't really properly got into contact with him. I feel quite desperate, and I can, after all, still do something else." This was said in a most peculiar tone, and when she was asked what she meant, whether perhaps she intended to disappear, she denied this, and replied, very mysteriously, " After all one can train oneself negatively! " Asked for an explanation, she whispers, half mysteriously, with a curious expression in her eyes: More than three years ago she attended a medical lecture in which there was mention of a youth of 18, who—entirely without self-reliance, completely wrapped up in his mother—never did anything. One night he crept into bed with his mother, had a fit of anxiety, and died. His body was examined by a hospital surgeon, who could find nothing wrong. The lecturer had concluded his lecture with the question, whether in relation to such a case one might not conceive of a negative training; the young man had absolutely no vital energy, and had trained himself for death. The whole idea which the patient has elaborated in this connexion seems absurd; however, it affords an opportunity of explaining to her that in her anxiety over her examination and her marriage she is once more seeking some new excuse. At last she laughs, quite delightedly, and we say good-bye; we are both going on a journey; she is going to the mountains with her mother, in order to rest a little before her final work for her examination. A little later she writes: she is having a dreadful time; she is suffering from terrible fits of anxiety; she is in mortal anguish. This condition began at home, before starting for the mountains, and on the way it got so much worse that she doesn't know what she will do. She is living with her mother in a villa; the mother is downstairs, and she is upstairs. There is a lantern in front of the house. At night she wakes up; the lantern has already been extinguished; so it is quite dark, and then a terrible fear comes over her; this is the beginning of the end! But—and for me this is the reassuring thing—although she is so weak that she thinks she is dying, she is nevertheless able to get up, take her clothes and a pillow, and go downstairs, at three o'clock in the morning, to wake the old lady from her sleep, weeping with terror; it is all up with her, she doesn't know what to do! At last her mother makes her lie on the sofa, and she falls asleep. This has happened repeatedly. During the day she is acting a part, or so it seems to her; there are several elderly ladies in the house who are delighted with her, while she herself cares absolutely nothing for society, and would rather be alone; then she cries, and the terrible sense of anxiety comes on; it is no use, it is all up with her, she is going to die.

She feels guilty, feels that she is spoiling her mother's holiday, and tries to persuade her to go away. A further letter: things are still going badly with her. On top of everything she heard that her fiancé had suddenly to undergo an operation for appendicitis. The operation was successful, but she was terribly worked up, and she is going home with her mother. She writes again, now at home: she went to see her fiancé in hospital; he is on the way to recovery, but she is in a frightful state; it is all up with her; she has terrible fits of anxiety; she feels that she is wasting away. In her anxiety she went to the doctor, and hinted at her trouble, but he did not understand her. On the advice of her mother and her fiancé she went to a neurologist, but again to no purpose. When can the consultations begin again? Perhaps they will help her, perhaps not; if it is too late she will no longer be here.

In every letter one notes a further contraction of the spiral. The clinical report which I receive speaks of the distracted appearance of the patient, who complained of the distressing feeling that her internal organs were gradually wasting away, whereas a thorough examination revealed absolutely nothing wrong. When the patient first comes to see me again she is very miserable; she is pale, with dark shadows under her eyes, and her glance is somewhat distracted. Weeping, she declares that she is having a miserable time; for sheer terror she doesn't know what to do; she can't even work, she has no belief in herself. When I suggest that she can after all postpone her examination again, that it is not too late to withdraw, she replied that she doesn't know what is going to happen about her marriage. Her fiancé is getting better, but is still in hospital, because the operation wound is not quite healed yet. She goes to see him every day, and then things aren't so bad with her. But if she is told anything depressing, anything about illness, and so on, she gets into the most frightful state about him, so that she has already said she would rather postpone her marriage. He is terribly good to her, he always consoles her, but he will no longer agree to a further postponement of their wedding. And she is so sorry for her mother, who has made all arrangements and has even seen to her trousseau; it seems so dreadful to tell her that nothing can come of it, that she won't any longer be there. Asked why she thought so, she replied, " I can feel how everything inside me is running down; it will soon come to that." The explanation that these ideas of self-destruction are due to her dread of the responsibilities of a permanent relation is accepted for the moment, but then she says, " No, I'm not convinced of that! "

Now she comes to me daily. She tells me that she is absolutely uninterested; that she makes arrangements about her trousseau, furniture, curtains, etc. as though for a stranger; always with the empty feeling: There's no sense in all this; what's the use? During an interview with her distracted mother, the latter suggests that the girl's condition is doubtless due to overwork, but it was quite impossible to get her to give up the examination. How is she to get married in this state? Her intended son-in-law, whom she has learnt to regard with increasing esteem, is still in hospital; he is touchingly affectionate and patient with her daughter, but she, the mother, is terribly anxious. It is explained to the excited woman that the new tasks which confront the girl are distressing her greatly, and that her nervous condition has been caused by this distress; one must try by forcible means to take the patient out of herself. To the mother, there seems a possibility of doing this, for as soon as the fiancé can leave the hospital he is to come to her house to be nursed for a little while. For the moment this is her best solution, while waiting to see how matters develop. Now the case is somewhat altered. The patient no longer declares that her internal organs are wasting away; she has now found a new idiom. She praises the patience and affection of her fiancé, and tells me of their plan—that he is to go to their house. When I ask her what she feels about this she replies: "That's the frightful thing, for something is happening to me, and when he comes out I shall become blind and deaf; I can often feel it coming on already." It is difficult to do anything with her. It has to be explained to her again and again that on the evidence of her case-history, of her development, she is a person who has never yet assumed any permanent obligation, a person whose sense of solidarity has never been developed, but that it is possible to make up for lost time. Behind all her symptoms is the terrible dread of surrendering her egocentricity, which it has hitherto been so easy for her to cherish; the dread of building up the relation between Me and You; the dread of responsibility. For hours at a time she is quite free from symptoms; then, suddenly, she relapses into her states of anxiety: "When he comes out I shall go blind and deaf!"

At last matters have gone so far that her fiancé comes to her mother's house, and she finds that she is neither blind nor deaf. But she is in a great state of excitement, and to some extent she translates this excitement into exaggerated care for him; only so can she carry on; but at all events this brings about the first diversion from her own person, which no longer quite mechanically takes precedence. Her mother realizes that she is now drastically taking herself in hand; one can see how hard she is trying. Here is a dream which she had at this time:

> She is in a canoe with a man and a married couple. She is feeling very nervous; she takes a revolver and fires at the water.

All her uncertainty, her anxiety in respect of her unknown future, are expressed in her dream, while at the same time we see the beginning of self-criticism; her symptoms are equivalent to a shot fired into the water!

After all her symptoms have been analysed again and again, she has to a great extent abandoned her deviations. But then she begins again: " Something frightful is going to happen! " I tell her that if she absolutely cannot imagine a state of community she ought to have the courage to dismiss her fiancé. But this she will not do. " That's just the dreadful thing; sometimes I think I can't live without him, but then again the very idea is frightful, I have a feeling of terror, and I would rather destroy myself." This too can be explained: she will not renounce him, since for him she represents the woman of a higher social class, to whom he looks up, and she is completely justified and authenticated by his devotion. So far she accepts him. But then the thought occurs to her: new duties, a responsible relation, limitation of her egocentricity, enlargement of her radius of action—and then she becomes afraid; then she becomes blind and deaf; unconsciously she endeavours to evade all obligations by cutting herself off completely from the outer world. Here again she behaves like the schoolgirl who, when she is unable to do anything, seeks cover behind the back of the child sitting in front of her; the protective back is now replaced by her symptoms. Further, she succeeds by her behaviour in causing her mother and her fiancé the greatest anxiety, which is an easy way of obtaining evidence of her value. These revelations are not without some effect. She comes to the conclusion that she will not sit for the examination, so at one point at all events she abandons her unconscious and spurious manœuvres. She would now be only too glad to escape from the devious courses into which she has strayed; but this is not so easy; we have to talk things over again and again, putting them into different shapes, with concrete examples. And a consultation with the fiancé becomes necessary. I am not unmindful of the fact that there might still be a question of postponing the marriage, but this would really leave things much as they were; for in that case she would do exactly what she has been doing for the past two years; she continues to evade difficulties by postponement, so that she simply goes round and round in a circle. It is quite possible that now—if matters are presented to her in a concise and inescapable form—she may summon up the courage to go ahead; on the other hand, she may try to escape through the expedient of a serious attack of illness. He, the fiancé, would be running a certain risk; it is for *him* to decide. He seems thoroughly to understand the situation; he knows exactly what is at stake, but he will not postpone the marriage, and hopes that all will go well.

The consultations were continued until just before the wedding. Now and again there were slight recurrences of the anxiety-states, but on the whole the patient was much calmer. At her wedding, a modest celebration in her family circle, the patient was very pale, but seemed to be contented enough, especially as she felt herself to be the focal point of the function. During her wedding-journey she sent me a postcard whose content seemed reassuring. A few months later her mother reported that the patient, who was no longer living in the city, had settled down happily in every way and was expecting a child. Later still the birth of a healthy boy was joyfully announced. A few months later still her husband informed me that his wife had quite lost all her morbid symptoms. The patient paid me a first personal visit eighteen months later, when she was able to introduce me to her little son, a fine boy, whom she wished as soon as possible to send to a Montessori kindergarten. To the query, " Would you be willing to part with him? " she replied, " If it's the right thing for him, of course, and after all, we are hoping for a second child." Since up to the advent of the second child, three years later, there had been no return of troubles of any sort, it may be hoped that the patient has finally overcome her difficulties.

Here again we have a case of a cossetted child who, in consequence of a ' mollycoddle ' education, did not grow up to be a courageous member of the community. She was always trying to gain reassurance, which she thought to achieve by shirking every sort of task. In this respect her circumstances were much against her. She was always able to draw back if anything was ' no longer any fun,' and to take up something else, in order to avoid a presumptive defeat. This was manifested in her relation to her fellow creatures, her intended profession, and her lover. With her mother, who, as she herself declared, lavished endless love and tenderness on her, she never became really intimate, although she reproached herself on this account—her old dodge of always excusing herself. Her inability to form close contacts had apparently been overcome when she met the man she finally married; which may be explained by the fact that being of a higher social status she was able to conjure up a feeling of superiority. This was evident in every kind of situation; as when she spoke of his inhibitions, or when she declared that she would run away if when she was married her sexual needs were not satisfied, or when during his temporary absence she humiliated him by forming another connexion. The same trend was manifested also in respect of sexual matters, as was to be observed even in her childhood; her making light of her own disabilities, but exaggerating those of others, and her defiant obstinacy, as when in her infancy, a baby with her bottle, she had decided for herself: ' Not just now.' All this was connected with a kind of cunning, which endeavoured always to get the upper hand. When her fiancé began to improve himself, thereby winning the sympathy of her relatives, who had previously been prejudiced against him, she found herself deprived of a hitherto effective argument, and delivered over to the ever-approaching bugbear of her examination and her wedding.

At this juncture she snatched at a notion derived from a lecture which she had heard years ago, the notion of 'negative training,' and twisted this into compulsive ideas which "displace the compulsive trend toward social regimentation" (Adler). The dynamic law of this patient, based on the experiences of early childhood, makes her avoid all sorts of tests and ordeals, and all responsibility; forcing her to think always only of herself and never of others; to want always to take and never to give. Her aim is to be the central point, to outshine all others, to have others look up to her as superior to them all; so that even in her obsessive thoughts of self-destruction she attributed godlike qualities to herself. Only when she had come quite clearly to realize the unsoundness of her way of life, only when she had plucked up sufficient courage to be ready to alter her attitude, was she able gradually to come to terms with her task in life, and assume responsibility for her actions.

(2)

A young architect, 31 years of age, whose exceptional talents, as I know, are greatly appreciated, complains that for a long while he has been suffering from lassitude, anxiety, and depression; he feels as though he were 'burnt out'; as though his initiative were paralysed, and he cannot work. Medical examinations have not revealed anything whatsoever. For the last three years he has been employed by a relative; the post does not suit him in any way; but he is incapable of making a change. This is all the more distressing inasmuch as he has been engaged to a young woman for the past four years, and cannot marry until he has a more assured livelihood.

It is to be noted that the patient, a tall, slender man, wearing spectacles with thick lenses, enters the room after he has first cautiously poked his head in at the door; and that he is extremely inhibited.

Questioned as to memories of his early childhood, he is

able to relate quite a number, all of which characterize him as of the visual type.

1. When he was 2 he went with his nurse and his sister—a year younger than himself—to pay a visit to his great-grandmother, who was half crazy, and who raged and jumped about the room. This did not impress him so greatly as did his little sister; he kept on looking at her and thinking: what a dear little girl she is!

It is surprising that the child was not particularly alarmed by the raving great-grandmother, and one may assume that there was a very strong bond between the children, since the boy unconsciously took refuge from the unpleasant situation by concentrating on the appearance of his little sister.

2. At 4 years of age, he was in the garden with his grandmother, his mother, and his aunts, when his mother suddenly fell down in a faint. He did not understand what was the matter, and collected some hairpins which had fallen out of her hair. This was held against him, and he was bitterly reproached because the incident had evidently made no impression on him. For many years he tortured himself with the notion that he was incapable of feeling.

In this second reminiscence the same tendency is expressed: the child turns away from an unpleasant situation by concentrating his attention on something else. Of course, this was done unconsciously, for he did not really understand what was happening: he could only judge from the agitated manner of his elders that it was something distressing. There is reason to suspect that the grown man will try to avoid anything unpleasant. One may assume also that the child was exceptionally sensitive; for his habit of torturing himself, and doubt as to whether he was capable of feeling, may very well be referred to the negative experience of having been unjustly accused of insensitiveness. It is also to be expected that the grown man will be very cautious and distrustful in his dealings with women.

3. At 5 and 6 years he listens to terrifying fairy-tales,

which the maidservant reads aloud; with the result that at night he is too frightened to sleep.

Evidence that the child was a sensitive, nervous, anxious type.

4. At the age of 10 his parents take him to look over a property which they are proposing to buy. When he says that he likes it very much his mother boxes his ears, because he was not asked for his opinion.

At table he is not allowed to speak unless he is spoken to; so he never of his own accord helps himself to anything; even to his favourite dishes; and this annoys his father.

The last two reminiscences show that the child suffered from constant repression, inflicted apparently by an unrestrained and authoritarian mother; that the way in which he was brought up robbed him of independence; that his father and mother had differences of opinion in respect of the principles of education; and that he apparently had to suffer as a result of these differences: all factors which must have contributed to make him subject to anxiety.

And now the preliminary history which the patient relates in a fragmentary fashion: he is the son of a wealthy wholesale merchant, who used to live in a large house with many servants, so that as a boy he was greatly spoiled. He has two sisters and a brother, the elder of the sisters is a year younger than he; his brother is three years, and the other sister five years his junior. As a young child he was extremely delicate, timid, and anxious; he suffered frequently from catarrh, his eyes were very sensitive, and from his tenth year his sight was defective. His parents' marriage was not a happy one; he realized this by the time he was ten or thereabouts, and the knowledge troubled him. His father is a man who likes to live well, to live and let live; his mother is excessively nervous, irritable, and authoritarian. After the first world war his parents separated; his father removed to another city, to which he transferred his business; he still often comes home on a visit, but his visits are seldom very enjoyable. The boy was his mother's darling; she lavished a great deal of attention upon him, and as he was delicate she even taught him herself during his first year at school. Always changeable in her moods, she would now treat him with excessive tenderness, and now with harshness and severity. Consequently the child's environment, as he grew up, was one of extreme contrasts; he was timid and shy, and was not allowed to play with strange children. For the elder of his two sisters he cherished an ardent affection; he passionately admired her, for she was the very opposite of himself; wild and youthful, afraid of no one, and holding her own even against her mother. As for his brother and the younger sister, he was and is rather indifferent to them.

When he was sent to school he was at once excused from the gymnastic class, as this would have entailed his arriving at the school as early as 7 a.m. He learned easily, was a very good scholar, and his schoolfellows thought well of him, especially as he was always ready to help them in their work.

He had no real friends, but always kept himself to himself. His favourite occupation was playing with toy bricks, so that at home he was often told "You will surely become an architect!"—and although as he grew older he took a great interest in languages, and thought of studying philology, he allowed his choice of a profession to be dictated by his parents. For some part of his years at school he lived with his grandmother, as his parents were living on their new estate. An aunt of his was living in his grandmother's house, and three girl cousins were frequent visitors; one was younger than he and two were older; of the oldest he was extremely fond. His parents, who themselves kept saddle-horses, wanted him to learn to ride. He could not be persuaded to do so; he was always afraid of horses; even as an adult he has not lost his fear of them.

After matriculating with credit he went to the university, when he had to leave home. He worked hard, and made friends; he was much interested in politics, and during this time, he thought, he was better able to get away from himself. Nevertheless, he still had anxiety-dreams.

As regards women, he was shy and distrustful. Apart from quite temporary relations with girls of a lower social status, who did not satisfy him, he had nothing to do with them. Sometimes he took a fancy to a woman of his own class, but then he set her on such a pedestal, and endowed her, in his imagination, with such admirable qualities, that he did not dare to approach her. Then his favourite sister married and left the district; he did not like her husband, and this distressed him. And now, shortly before the date of his examination, he had to undergo his term of military service, and the idea of it filled him with horror. He had been going about for weeks with a cough of which he could not get rid, and suddenly he began to spit blood.

On his doctor's advice he went up into the mountains. After two months there he was better; he went back to his former mode of life, smoked a great deal, swam, and went on exhausting walking tours, until he had a hæmorrhage. For months he lay in bed; then he was given a pneumothorax, but it gave way. After a year in a sanatorium he pressed the doctor to give him leave to sit for his final examination. For two months he studied in the university city, and then sat for the examination, which he did not find difficult. It was to have taken five days; on the evening of the fourth day he had a serious hæmorrhage. Again he was months in bed; then he was transferred to a Swiss sanatorium, where in the course of eighteen months two serious operations were performed. Altogether, illness and treatment had taken up six years of his life; the last year was spent entirely in the sanatorium. When his condition permitted he had continued to work, both at his speciality and at general subjects. Three years ago he was so far restored that he was able to sit for his examination again, and then make a beginning in the profession which he still wishes to follow.

During his last year in Switzerland he made the acquaintance of the young woman who is now his fiancée; she had spent some months in the sanatorium on account of a nervous asthma. She was a foreigner; her people were manufacturers; she had lost her mother some years previously, and was living a joyless family life, against which she secretly rebelled, with an embittered and despotic father and a number of brothers and sisters. Although she was a member of a liberal profession she did not practise it, but wasted her life in quarrels with her father and attacks of asthma, which became less troublesome only when he was away from home. The first approach came from her; she sought my patient's company, and engaged in long discussions with him; and although in every respect they were absolutely different—in their views of the world in general, their inclinations, and their tastes—they gradually conceived an affection for each other. Again at her initiative they became sexually intimate, and an engagement followed. From the very outset he had doubts as to whether this woman was really the right wife for him. However, she so fully recognized his intellectual superiority, professing that she was willing to be guided by him, that he constantly tried to overlook the doubts evoked by her supersensitiveness, her claims upon his person, and modes of behaviour that seemed to him childish and immature. There were times when he was content, when he looked forward to a happy future spent together, but these peaceful days did not long continue; the old excitement and irritability returned, which were really more than he could stand. Then, since she was better, she had to go home, only to be prostrated for weeks by a severe attack of asthma. My patient also, his cure completed, returned home a few months later. Since his younger brother, who did not get on with his mother, had now left home, while his younger sister, who had also felt oppressed by her mother, had escaped from her by insisting upon the necessity of a professional education, their mother now had her darling son to herself, and immediately devoted herself to looking after him. She found him the position he now held in his relative's office, but he took absolutely no interest in the work. He is carrying on a lively correspondence with his fiancée, and every year she visits him for weeks at a time. At first they were delighted to be together, but then they both suffered from the mother's petty jealousy; and finally the old agitation and friction returned, with disputes, and fits of anger, and tearful scenes of reconciliation. He sometimes visited his fiancée in her home, but felt so uncomfortable there that he was glad to leave. A few months ago, when his fiancée again came to stay with him, she asked him urgently to marry her. But he is not yet in a position to marry; however, he has promised her that he will try to obtain a better position, that there may be an end of this unsatisfactory state of affairs. And now his conscience is always troubling him, because he is doing nothing of the kind; he feels paralysed, and does not know what is going to happen.

We discuss his relation to his mother. She is easily offended, feels herself neglected, torments him and tries, by her care of him, to obtain complete control over him. He must not go out in the evening lest he should catch cold; she does not like the friend who sometimes comes to see him; she is, as he puts it, a " mother by the grace of God." Asked whether he has never thought of asserting his independence and living alone, he replies that he " cannot do that to his mother "; she would think him a bad son if he refused to live with her. Everything is unsatisfactory; he does his work reluctantly, receives a daily letter from his fiancée, writes his daily letter to her, and goes to bed. He sleeps badly, and has oppressive dreams; he has just remembered a fantasy which has occurred to him repeatedly of late when he has been half asleep.

He sees before him large dark grey discs; he thinks he is going to fall on to them; he struggles to escape and wakes with a start, feeling terrified.

The grey colour of the discs, the struggle to escape a threatening fate, the terror on waking, show the desperate nature of his situation.

We have repeatedly discussed his relation to his fiancée. There is a complete dichotomy in his feelings for her; he feels that he loves her, yet it seems to him that he could not possibly live with her. Asked how he loves her, whether as a woman or as a human being, he replies: " As a child." He still hopes to remould her, but then the contrast between them seems insuperable. Again he complains of his life with his mother. Through intensive discussions of his development in early childhood he is gradually made to realize that he to-day, as a grown man, is just as dependent on his mother, just as tied to her, as in his early childhood. Then he could not behave otherwise than as he did, for he had not learnt to grapple with a difficult situation; but to-day, as a man with individual values and faculties, he must gradually contrive to use these and become an independent person. Despite his great intelligence, the patient would find it very difficult to pull himself out of his conditioned attitude and begin to build up an independent life. His first attempt was to go out in the evening, and although his mother made objections and sat up, unhappy and offended, until he returned late at night, he continued to go out, although his conscience reproached him.

He is thankful that he has for once had it out with his mother, and has told her that he cannot possibly continue to live as he was living; that he must go out. And that is that! He sees also that it would help his mother if she were to understand how her obstinacy has driven her husband and all her children away.

After this first success with his mother his attitude towards his fiancée becomes more decisive. He has now written to her telling her that of course he loves her, but that they cannot marry until they have both changed. In support of his assertion he has adduced a number of incidents from the last few years, showing how they have tormented each other. He now sees that the guilt was on both sides. He now has to be shown that one cannot speak of guilt, but only of error; that on account of his experiences as a young child he has not sufficient confidence to take the shaping of his life into his own hands, and in the case of his fiancée also the circumstances of her development have contributed to discourage her. As though in confirmation she writes a despairing letter: " I will change myself, but do you have confidence in me, or I can have none in myself! " He is torn to and fro by his emotions, and does not know what he should do, for she has so often made such promises, and things remain just the same.

He now suggests that she too might be interested in individual-psychology, but she does not agree.

A dream of this period:

> He finds himself in a large room; he is being followed or he is looking for something. The room grows narrower, and narrower, until only a large pipe is left, through which a light is glimmering. He wants to get out, and tries with all his might to do so, crawling on hands and knees.

The light glimmering into a narrow room; there is the new realization, thanks to individual-psychology's way of looking at things, by which his neurotically restricted life is to be enlarged. The dream also shows plainly the first tendency toward greater activity, which is, as a matter of fact, now showing itself; in respect of his mother and his fiancée, and in his profession, for he is beginning to take steps toward obtaining another position.

His correspondence with his fiancée worries him greatly. She writes illogically, with false sentimentality, as he puts it, and reproaches him; and he finds himself in a wavering mood. Now he feels that he must not break a promise once given; but then he remembers the many unpleasantnesses which arise during her visits; her constant irritability, and the nagging complaints by which she paralyses his creative powers.

Another dream:

> He is standing on the highway; he sees a lorry, travelling at a great speed. On the lorry are sitting soldiers, with rifles and fixed bayonets; there is a girl among them.

> *He thinks to himself: there is something (political) happening in the town again; but he remains quite indifferent.*

As an appendix to this, another dream:

> *He is struggling on the floor with a maidservant, and is greatly excited.*

He is so aloof, so abstracted, that things which he used to find of the greatest interest (political activity) make no impression on him. In the dream he considers the sexual problem: there is a state of war (hostile attitude toward women). On further discussion he admits that as a very young man he had homosexual tendencies. So, the homosexual tendencies, the attraction toward girls of a lower class (he calls to mind a particular connexion, and then other women, whom he placed on pedestals, so that they too were not the right partners for him)—all this is passing. He will have to adopt a new attitude toward women.

The correspondence with his fiancée is continued: she is stubborn and importunate. It is clear to him that she wishes to compel him to marry her, in order that she may escape from her empty, unprofitable and oppressed existence. At the same time he sees clearly that he has given his fiancée—in his imagination—the qualities which he would wish her to possess; but that as a matter of fact this marriage would mean only a continuation of the maternal regime—that in his dread of life he would merely have fled from one cage into another. Having realized this, he declares: "I must make an end of excuses and write to her honestly saying that I don't any longer wish to marry."

The wavering attitude which persists in spite of this masculine gesture is shown by a dream:

> *He sees the head of his fiancée, but with beautiful fair hair, which she does not possess in reality, and the parting is on the opposite side to that on which she is accustomed to make it.*

That is, he imagines her as he would like to have her, with a different attitude to life.

The negotiations in respect of a new post are continuing. He has established connexions which may be of great assistance to him, and although nothing is yet settled he ventures, against his mother's will, to give his present employer notice. Now he goes through a bad time. His fiancée is not satisfied; she writes to his mother, telling how miserable she is; that he no longer loves her. His mother treats him with consideration, as though he were an invalid, but he thinks that he can perceive signs of a certain satisfaction (because she now has him to herself again). A letter is received from a woman friend of his fiancée; his conscience gives him no rest; he has pains in the chest and catarrh; but he is glad that he has written the truth to her. Here is a dream:

> He is pursued by a little girl, again through a narrow gangway. He knows nothing more, except that an individual-psychological idea occurred to him, and his pursuer vanished like a ghost.

His fiancée is a little girl; on the one hand, she is actually small; on the other, he regards her as a child, from whose attentions he can free himself with the help of individual-psychological analyses. Also, he is not yet independent of help; he grasps at individual-psychology in order to escape the pursuing spectre.

But this is a curious thing: he declares that he is tormented by contrary impulses, yet he is so profoundly satisfied by the turn things are taking that he is sometimes quite cheerful, in comparison with his former state.

His fiancée ventures on a last attempt; she asks him to meet her half-way, in a neighbouring town, in order to talk things over. He sees the trap—she knows that if they were to meet face to face he might not be able to hold out—and refuses to meet her. He has a dream:

> He is lying on his bed, on which his fiancée is sitting. She weeps and lays her head on his breast. He kisses her hand and says, "I don't love you," and he wakes with a sense of satisfaction.

In the dream he compels himself to do what he has so far

been incapable of doing in real life: to remain resolute when face to face with his fiancée.

Another day he is excited when he comes to see me: he has to decide whether he will accept a position abroad, one which offers him great chances. If he hesitates it is on his mother's account: he would have to leave her quite alone. He has a dream:

> He is pursued; he passes through a dark room, then through a lighted room into another dark room. At last he seems to come to a tower, and rises without going up any steps, until he reaches a pedestal on which his mother is lying in her night-dress. She has white hair (actually she is a blonde). He is trying to cover her with a blanket when he wakes in distress.

The three rooms through which he is pursued are: the dark past, the brighter present (for at the moment he feels encouraged) and the dark future which lies before him. He is afraid of the unknown; he rises (the chances which are offered to him) without going up any steps; by which his uncertainty is increased; and he sees, on a pedestal, his mother, greatly aged and lying, as it were, in her shroud. He feels tenderness for her, as is shown by his covering her with a blanket; at the same time he feels guilty, for he knows that he has left her alone, and that this desertion will be the death of her. When he realizes that the purpose of the dream is to encourage his despondency, and that his regard for his mother signifies a pretext for evading the responsibility of living his own life, he decides to accept the new post. Here is a dream:

> With a great company of young people (mostly relations) he is bathing in the sea, which is beautiful and full of glorious colours. They swim out to sea, and at last they come to a coast-line: South America. On the beach is a covered hall painted in brilliant colours; from this one goes into a second and a third hall. Suddenly they all dance, and his younger sister plays the piano. A somewhat nervous feeling comes over him, and he looks out of

> the window to see whether any natives are in sight. He sees a crowd of savages and hears Spanish being spoken; he gathers the young people together, shouting that above all his little sister must be rescued. So they must fly! Suddenly of the whole crowd of natives only a mulatto is left, who is conversing in cultured tones with one of the young people. They rush into the sea, which suddenly is not the sea at all, but a very beautiful green meadow, which is, however, very moist, and one rather sinks into it. He wakes with a feeling of rapture.

During the consultation he states that he has only quite recently realized his delight in colour; formerly he took pleasure only in form. The scene of the dream (the sea-coast) reminds him of many visits to relatives who live at the seaside. The dream represents an argument with himself. It shows the carefree life in the bosom of his family, the awakening of the spirit of enterprise (his student years) and an adventurous landing in a remote foreign country, a thing for which he often longed during his periods of extreme depression. However, he enters a covered hall—that is, he is again protected. The presence of his sister emphasizes the solidarity of the family, but at the same time it points to the awakening sense of responsibility; for just recently there has been a great deal of talk about his little sister, and he is worried about her education. Despite all his timidity he plays a heroic part, although in the end they take to flight. The whole dream displays activity, which is a recent acquisition, while at the same time he carries his former attitude *ad absurdum*; exaggerating dangers. First there was a horde of savages, but then only a single mulatto was left, who conversed in a cultivated fashion; then they think to plunge into the bottomless ocean, but it is really a beautiful green meadow into which they sink a little. So he is not yet entirely courageous! But the dream, with its bright colours, points to a preparation for life, especially when one compares it with the grey, oppressive colourless atmosphere of the first dream.

He has now finally told his fiancée that they must go their several ways. And he insists that notwithstanding all attacks of anxiety and sentimentality, he will show his teeth to life and will consciously go about the business of reshaping it on his own responsibility.

I heard from him at long intervals. He was still working very hard, for his professional activities, under completely different circumstances, were extremely exacting; but he was making his way; he was entrusted with big jobs, and was equal to them. About two years after the end of his treatment he wrote at some length; he had met a woman whom he loved and who made him happy. A notice of their wedding followed, and a year later the joyful news that to their great delight a child had been born to them.

Portrait of the Patient. A nervous, delicate child with sensitive respiratory organs and defective sight is, on the one hand, brought up in an over-indulgent manner, and overwhelmed with tenderness, so that he does not learn to be independent. On the other hand, he is kept under strict and authoritarian control—the best way of making a man timid and uncertain, of suppressing any growth of self-confidence, and prematurely sapping his active energies. The disharmony of his parents' marriage, the circumstance of being surrounded only by women of different generations, most of whom spoiled him, have contributed to enhance his hesitating attitude toward life (remember his way of cautiously putting his head in at the door on the occasion of his first visit) and to make him distrustful, afraid, and uncertain in his relation to women, though always—as in the case of his mother—seeking tenderness and fearing rejection. Pursued by anxiety, he shirks all responsibility, has always to cling to others, and allows them to determine his actions. This is shown in his recollections, in respect of the position of his sister, and in his choice of a profession, to which latter, however, a marked over-compensation for defective sight (aptitude for appreciating forms and figures) may have contributed. The beginning of tuberculosis coincides with the time when he was depressed by the marriage of his favourite sister and was greatly dreading the period of military service. In view of the susceptibility of the respiratory organs, the psychic factors might have favoured the incidence of the disease, which for years deprived him of the power of shaping his life. He met a woman who apparently admired him, but at the same time completely dominated him by her demands and caprices. It was she who brought about a sexual relation and thereby compelled him to become engaged to her. Despite all misgivings and negative experiences, he remained in the same dependence upon her as marked his relations with his mother. Unconsciously, however, he rebelled through his symptoms, his lassitude and fits of depression, his lack of resolution, and his inability to work, which made it impossible for him to secure a better position; so that his marriage could be constantly postponed.

On the basis of his childish experiences this adult human being had constructed his dynamic law: " Never to run any risk, to avoid the front line of life; best of all, to remain in the nursery! "

When he had come to understand his style of life, and had taken the first steps which seemed to promise success, he was ready to set to work on effecting a serious change, to reconstruct his life completely, and to become a responsible member of the community.

VI

The Problem of the Application of Individual-psychological Therapy[1]

HERE was a case of a woman of 30, who was referred to me for individual-psychological treatment by a doctor, with the diagnosis: "Fits of depression resulting from a continual conflict." She had come from abroad; for some two months her personal affairs would keep her in the city, and she wanted, when they were settled, to go abroad again. She was to profit in the interval by undergoing treatment, although it was clear to us—to the doctor and myself—that in so short a time her treatment could hardly be completed; still, it might be possible to lay down a basis from which further progress could be made.

My first impression of her was that here was a truly desperate woman. The patient was extremely excited; she spoke loudly, almost in a shrieking voice, wept at intervals, and excused her behaviour by saying that she had just received some very bad news. In order to make the situation intelligible I had better first relate the previous history of the patient, which I learned gradually during the first few interviews.

The patient was born in what was formerly Russian Poland, and comes of a good middle-class family. She is a second child, having two brothers, one three years older than she and one three and a half years younger. Of her parents she says that when she was a little child her mother was not so close to her as her father; she was a much more serious character, while he—although a business man—always found time to give to the children, and was a very affectionate parent. She describes her father as a good-natured but very superficial and unintellectual man. Her development

[1] Published in *Int. Zeitschr. für Individualpsychologie, Vienna,* 15th year, vol. I.

in early childhood was fairly normal. She was very delicate; in her early childhood she had whooping-cough and measles, and often suffered from feverish affections of the respiratory organs. Even as a fairly young child she was keenly observant and critical in her attitude to everything. So it very soon became apparent to her that her parents' marriage was not a happy one. She was aware of the tension under which they lived, and secretly she was more and more inclined to take her mother's side, at the same time becoming increasingly estranged from her father. Her mother now attracted her more and more; for the child she was the representative of another world; she was fragile, sensitive, and very intellectual; " she ought really to have been a student," said the patient, who thought she herself was very like her mother.

The elder brother was very talented; later on he was also very diligent, and made something of himself. He had always oppressed her, while the younger brother, whom she described as " a quiet scholarly character," was her close companion. She did well at school; she was very ambitious, and consciously tried not to fall behind her elder brother, concerning whom she always had the feeling that her parents preferred him to her; moreover, he had always behaved as though he himself were convinced of this. She did not bear her little brother a grudge because he was favoured as the youngest.

The patient described herself as a thoughtful child, who could be very gay at times, but who suffered from extreme emotional ups and downs. She did well in the gymnasium also; and was always a good comrade. Puberty was for her a difficult time; she read a great deal and had fits of melancholy. In view of her parents' marriage she had thought a great deal about the mutual relation of the sexes, and she was quite resolved that there could be no question of marriage for her without complete intellectual and spiritual communion. About this time a friend of her elder brother began to frequent the house; as a student he spent his holidays with the family. They were together day after day; they studied literature, history, and the history of art together; they lived in an intellectual world, and had high ethical ideals. It often occurred to her that perhaps marriage to this man might be possible. One day he disappeared without taking his leave, and she saw no more of him. The fact that he could treat her so caused her great suffering; she felt depreciated; but was too proud to say anything. During the next holidays he appeared again, but she was too hurt to get into touch with him. Years later he met her once again, and confessed that he had always loved her alone. He had drawn back then because he was afraid of arousing feelings in her which he might perhaps be unable fully to satisfy.

She matriculated with credit, and wanted to study philology; to do this she would have to go to the capital. About this time—she was 18 or 19 years of age—she altered her opinions. Body and intellect are two different things; now she conceded that the body has rights of its own. And now she made the discovery that she, who was so passionately interested in intellectual, ethical, and moral problems, was especially attracted by men who were the absolute antithesis of her ideals. She remembered that she had been particularly fascinated by a student who had the reputation of being particularly brutal, and a woman-hunter; for whom women were merely females. She believed that she would certainly have entered into sexual relations with him if they had not happened to quarrel just about that time. She continued her studies with enthusiasm. When she had concluded her fourth semester her father died. She was aware that this event did not greatly affect her, for she had become quite estranged from her father mentally, and had drawn closer and closer to her mother.

Her financial situation had undergone such a change that she decided to abandon her studies for the time being and try to earn some money, in the hope of resuming her studies later on. She was very glad to obtain a post in a great international organization, especially as it afforded her an opportunity of doing journalistic work. She had been six months in this post when a new colleague made his appearance, a man who had fascinated her even when she had observed him only from a distance. She saw that in every respect he was superior to her other colleagues, and she was enraptured when an opportunity occurred of making his personal acquaintance. His intellectual brilliance was dazzling, and so fascinated her that she was delighted when he sought to enter into closer relations with her. It was not long before a passionate love affair had developed between them. She lived in a state of intoxication, for here all that she had imagined as regards the ideal relation with a man was exquisitely realized.

He was thirty years of age. He told her that he was a widower. It gradually came out that he, who had been greatly oppressed at home, had broken away when he was a nineteen year old student, inasmuch as against the will of his parents he had entered into an unofficial marriage with a girl of eighteen. They had a hard struggle; after a year of their life together a girl child was born, and four years later a second girl. But about this time they ceased to live together; he loved his wife indeed as a human being, but as a woman she no longer satisfied him. In the meantime he had made the acquaintance of a married woman, and fell in love with her. From this time onwards he found his wife's company intolerable. He left her, and fled with the second woman, whom he desired as a *woman,* to Roumania. His happiness did not last long, for he found that this woman did not speak the truth and since, as he said, he was "a fanatic for the truth," he could not endure this fault, and he left her. Now followed a period of various fleeting relations, which did not satisfy him, for he wanted something more. His first wife, who was always very delicate, could not get over the loss of her husband; she fell ill and died, and the children were sent to her parents.

After listening to this narrative my patient once ventured,

very timidly, to confess to the man the doubt whether *she* would be able to satisfy him. However, he dispelled her doubts by assuring her that in her he had found the synthesis, that for him she represented his highest ideal as *woman* and as *human being,* so that their relation was indissoluble. She would now have liked to introduce him to her family, for she was convinced that he would make the same impression on them as on her. And now she suffered a disappointment, for her mother, as well as her two brothers (as the elder showed openly, and the younger more cautiously) took a dislike to the man. Her mother, as a matter of fact, had a misgiving which she did not quite openly confess to her daughter. She knew only that the man was a widower, and she tried to justify her misgiving by arguing that her daughter, a girl of 22, definitely ought not to marry a widower with two daughters. For my patient the idea of leaving the man was unthinkable; and since at this juncture he was transferred, within the same organization, to a South German capital, they were married. The children now came home to their father; two girls, of 10 and 6 years of age. Their relations with their new mother were excellent, and a few years of unbroken happiness followed. Again and again the patient wrote to her mother telling her how happy she was; she was always trying to prove that her mother had been mistaken. Now she would have had an opportunity of continuing her studies, and often thought of doing so; she spoke about it, but never did anything. Two years ago she contracted influenza, after which a tubercular catarrh of the apices of the lungs developed. A pneumothorax had to be resorted to; after which she had a severe attack of pleurisy, which involved a very long period of medical attendance and nursing. She felt that it was only the love and care which her husband lavished on her that enabled her to recover from this serious illness. Some time after this she became pregnant; but her pregnancy had to be terminated, as owing to the state of her health she could not be allowed to bear a child. This was a great grief to her. Three months later her husband was appointed to Berlin; still working in the same organization. They were all very glad of this, and it seemed as though the move would facilitate the education of the children. They went to Berlin, found accommodation, sent the younger child to school, and took steps to enable the elder girl to continue the course of social education which she had already begun. Her husband was then suddenly summoned for three months to the city in which she had first met him. She was left alone with the children; she lived a very solitary life, for she knew no one in Berlin, and only waited for his letters; for since their marriage they had never yet been separated. He told her in his letters how he longed for her, and after a month of separation he simply had to come to her, at least for a day; again she was perfectly happy with him. On the occasion of this visit he told her about a very interesting woman whom he had met. She was quite unsuspicious; she was so completely convinced of his love that she listened to his description of this woman with the same interest that she felt in anything that concerned him. He went back to the city in which they had first met; the conference continued to sit; and after a few weeks he wrote to her saying that he loved this woman. For him there was no dilemma; she was and remained his ideal. She did not know what to make of this confession; they continued to write to each other, and he was still the same. Then came another letter; he had struggled for a long time, but there was nothing to be done about it—he and this woman loved each other and they were now living together. Though there could be no question of that for them now (for him and my patient) they were still indissolubly bound to each other, for their relation was so firmly anchored, so unbreakable, that they simply made *one* big family.

Although my patient must really have been prepared for this, the news was a terrible blow to her. She tried to keep the truth from the children, since she did not wish to expose their father to them, and in a state of great excitement she went to see him. There was a scene; it was impossible to come to an understanding with him, for he insisted that he was depriving her of nothing; she was still his ideal; but he was bound to live with the other woman, especially as she was expecting a child. This was, of course, the worst of all for her; it reopened an old wound. In despair she returned to Berlin, and made an unsuccessful attempt at suicide. The doctor who was called in was very humane. He saw in what a desperate situation this woman found herself, who on account of her illness was still in need of the greatest care and consideration, and he sent a woman acquaintance of his to see her, a woman who was actively engaged in social and welfare work. One day this woman introduced herself to my embittered and despairing patient, who was lying in bed and weeping incessantly. It was a new experience for her, that a perfect stranger should come to her and—apparently in the most tactful manner—take an interest in her troubles. So matters stood for some time, until at last a convalescent home was found in which she could have medical attention at a moderate price. As we have seen, her relations with the children were excellent; but for both parties it was painful, and very difficult, to do the right thing in such a situation. The children idolized their father, regarding him as an exceptional person to whom the generally accepted laws did not apply. They could not therefore accuse him, but they loved their new mother too, and saw how grievously she was suffering. In this dilemma the best thing for the patient was, of course, to leave Berlin. The doctor, indeed, thought it of great importance, in view of the state of her lungs, that she should spend some time in a sanatorium. Before this could be arranged a number of preliminaries were necessary, which were already receiving the attention of the lady who was interested in her case. It might, however, be some considerable time before the permit was obtained, so that in the meantime her friends were thankful to be able to send her to the convalescent home. In respect of her psychic condition it had not done her much good; she had fits of depression, never did anything, and only brooded over her unhappiness. Her husband was fully informed as to her condition, for during this period she corresponded with him through the doctor. After she had been abroad for some weeks she returned to Berlin. Various matters had to be settled, and the material problem played an important role. Her husband was apparently very anxious about her, but was unpunctual in the dispatch of remittances, although the younger daughter had to be provided for; in the meantime the elder girl was doing practical work in a foreign nursing-home. The question of sending the patient to a sanatorium had by now become more acute; but it might be another two months before she could go, and for these two months the patient was to remain here under treatment. On the day when she first came to me she had just received the news that her husband had become a father; hence her excited condition.

The patient found it very difficult to take her mind off her troubles. Here is a recollection of her childhood:

> She is four years old, sitting on a bedroom chamber; she is alone in the room; the door is closed. In the adjoining room her mother and her elder brother are attending to the younger boy, who will not eat his gruel. The elder brother has a habit of describing the day's events in little verses, which he intones. He suddenly rushes into the room in which she is sitting, with a line for which he had only with difficulty found the last word; he sings the line to her, and she at once finds the required word. He will not believe that she has found the word on the spur of the moment; he thinks she is lying; she must have heard what they were saying in the next room, including the final word; but this is not the case. She is extremely indignant at this injustice and suspicion.

What does this reminiscence tell us?

There is the child, sitting by herself in a room whose door is closed. The others (the outer world) are together outside, attending to the little brother. Here, already, one sees the contrast: the patient feels herself quite isolated, not rooted in the family; everything turns upon the little boy. And now the outer world (the brother) comes in to her, but in a hostile sense, in order to depreciate her achievement; in order to suspect her unjustly; in order to do something to her against which she is bound to protest. A vivid light is thrown on the child's whole situation. From this reminiscence we can see that the child felt herself to be very insecure in her community, that she confronted life distrustfully and timidly; further, one can even assume that this person might become a fanatic for truth and justice.

The patient was obliged to confirm this: "Yes, she had always been timid"; and various other memories were recalled; how as a child she suffered for a long time from the fear that a tile might fall on her; and after she learned of the existence of bacteria there was a time when she thought she was endangered by them. Further, she remembered that when she was a schoolgirl she once overheard a conversation in the course of which there was apparently some talk of a paralytic, who could neither walk nor speak; she became terribly afraid of what would happen if she should be paralysed; and she lay motionless and moved her lips without making a sound, in order to see whether people could understand her. She also confirmed the fanatical love of truth; she was never able to tell a lie; and her strict sense of justice, which often assumed quite ridiculous forms: for example, even to-day, when she is brushing her teeth, she cannot brush the upper teeth more than the lower, and vice versa. We spoke of her ambition at school; how the thought was always present that she must not fall behind her brother.

In our interviews it was at first impossible to keep to the subject under discussion. She always reverted to her sufferings; she had been so utterly bound up with her husband, and she could not break away from him. This was terribly distressing, as her thoughts could not escape from the vicious circle: "For eight years I knew and loved him; how could he do this to me? Is he a scoundrel? But could I have loved him if he had been a scoundrel? How could I? " And so she continued, going round and round in a circle. When I asked her if she was divorced (I did not know whether she was) she denied it with horror; she would never divorce him.

We began the treatment with an analysis of the husband. This was followed by an objective examination, and she realized that she had seen everything quite differently from what it really was. She began—step by step—to contrast herself with him in a critical spirit; to perceive his unreliability, his vanity, and the arrogance with which he always claimed special privileges for himself; his impatience, his intolerance of any opinion but his own.

Now too she remembered that at the beginning of her acquaintance with him she had had very serious misgivings on account of his behaviour to women; that—consciously or unconsciously—she had tempered her usually critical regard, and in so doing had distorted the truth. In this connexion she suddenly remembered that in South Germany, at the time when she alleged that she was perfectly happy, she once puzzled for months over the question (which she had absolutely forgotten) whether it would not be better for them to separate, since she could not endure his depreciatory tactics—which he sometimes employed against herself—but then again there were periods of the greatest happiness. And so gradually the picture was filled out, until she understood that all these modes of behaviour were not 'scoundrelism,' but typical characteristics of a neurotic person. From this point it was not difficult to proceed to self-analysis, and to make her understand why, or rather 'to what end,' she was forced to behave thus or thus. She could not have seen clearly what she was doing, for otherwise she could not have continued this relation, which brought her for the first time what she had hitherto striven for in vain: complete authentication! *He* was as necessary to *her* as *she* was to *him*; since for him too she had the greatest, most uncritical admiration. Of course, this realization came to her only slowly and hesitatingly. There were hours when she could be roused only for a moment from her mood of depression; at other times she co-operated, disputed, contradicted, and at last agreed. She complained greatly of her condition; she coughed, and slept badly, and described how, on waking, a feeling as though an ice-cold hand were gripping her heart reminded her of her misery.

It was very necessary that she should have some occupation, and fortunately it was possible to arrange for her to work half the day as a voluntary helper in a social welfare organization. She had some difficulty in resolving to undertake this work, for she had not the least remnant of self-confidence, but at last she ventured to begin, and with that she had taken a step forward. For her, as a foreigner, the work was particularly arduous, but it was a task for which she, with her great intelligence and quick understanding, was very well fitted. She found that she could do the work excellently, and to the satisfaction of her chiefs. She was even told that she was doing better than experienced workers. This encouraged her for the time being, but hours of profound depression followed her moments of elation. Moreover, her husband, who hitherto had always kept up appearances, now became very neglectful. The tone of his letters was uninterested, and he was unpunctual in sending remittances; he had, after all, to provide for the other woman and her child. She was often without money, and did not know where she could borrow some until the next remittance arrived. Once, when I suggested that she could perhaps apply to the relevant department of the organization in which her husband was working, she rejected my advice with horror: "For God's sake, no; no one must know about it!" She felt that what was happening was such a disgrace, she felt so dishonoured by the fact that such a thing could happen to *her,* that she would rather put up with the present state of things than disclose it in the quarter to which she might look for a settlement of her difficulties. Even so, she could not make up her mind to write to her husband in drastic terms about this question of money; he must not think her a 'calculating' woman. Naturally, advantage was taken of these incidents, and therapeutic use was made of them.

She was still corresponding with her mother, who for the last two years had been living in Palestine with her younger son, and always in such terms that appearances were preserved. She wrote to her only at long intervals, and professed to be very unhappy, as her mother was ill, and worried about her.

On the whole, some progress was perceptible; and the patient was co-operating properly at our interviews. Although she had now adopted the formula that where her husband was concerned nothing could now surprise her, that she was prepared for anything, she was none the less always badly upset if one of his rare letters contained a slighting remark.

Here is a dream from the time when she was first beginning to make progress:

> She is sitting in a circle of the friends of her youth; all are looking pale, ill, and depressed. Then she says: "How could he, who made such a brief appearance here, do us all such a grievous wrong?"

In short: she begins to emerge from her isolation, and gets into touch with her fellow-creatures; but, indeed, only with those of whom she knows that they liked her before; and, after all, only in so far as *her* grief is the grief of the community.

Now and again it happens that she thinks: "Sometimes I think, after all, I can get over it; but then it seems as though it would be impossible." She has attacks of terror in the street; she thinks there is a man behind her; that she might be followed, beaten up, shot.

All her fear of humanity, her distrust of men, arising from the earliest experiences of her childhood, find expression in these anxiety-phantasies. And then she happens to go to a lecture; a courageous impulse. Unfortunately she meets there an acquaintance, coming from her home town, who speaks to her. She leaves the woman suddenly, and takes to flight; she might have been questioned about her husband. Time and time again we have talked these matters over, and found the red thread that is always reappearing: the dread of humiliation, of disgrace!

A little further progress is made: after prolonged discussion she plucks up courage to write to her mother, telling her the truth; though for a long while she tried to put off writing the letter, because she was afraid the agitation caused by learning the truth might endanger her mother's life. This excuse also is exposed as a measure of self-defence. We even get so far as to discuss her future prospects, in view of the fact that she is perfectly capable of reconstructing her life, and even finding a new happiness. She contradicts me; she will not hear of it, she rejects the idea in alarm; nevertheless, she thinks the matter over, as is shown by a dream of this period:

> She is with her husband, and there is a child also; not his own, but one he has adopted. At the same time she sees another husband, to whom she belongs, a man who is really the husband of one of her acquaintances, whom actually she believes to be very happily married. The conversation turns upon the child, who is to be adopted by the new husband, but he is willing only to take the child in, and not to adopt it.

So she is considering the problem; and the longing for a child is also expressed in the dream. " It is not his own child! " So she will not have it that his child (the child of that other woman) is really his own child. At the same time the dream shows the dread of forming a new connexion, and reveals her distrust of men (she lets it seem that a man belongs to her of whom she knows that he is happily married). In the dream, too, she compares her husband with the other man, and finds that the other is ' petty and commonplace '; so she cannot yet break away from her husband.

But as a matter of fact she is trying to break away from the past, with more or less success.

Then comes a letter from her mother; she is glad to have learned the truth; she had long suspected that things were not going well with her daughter. She is overcome by a great longing for her mother; she would like best of all to go to her, but in her situation that is impossible; besides, her people are finding it very difficult to pay their way. Still, she seriously considers the idea of going to join her mother later on; she wishes that she could make sufficient progress to obtain the permit to go to the sanatorium. But physically she is in a pitiful condition. As she is always financially embarrassed, she cannot feed herself up as she ought to do; it has been a very cold winter, and her room was not sufficiently heated. She had a bad cough and was always running a temperature. At last she was informed that arrangements had been made for her to undergo a prolonged cure at the sanatorium. And now she began to plan how she could make use of her spare time; she could make a thorough study of languages, read through a course of psychological literature, and generally increase her store of learning. But first, of course, all sorts of things had to be seen to, and her husband wanted to come here and help her. She longed for him intolerably, and for some time she wavered. We discussed the pros and cons, but naturally the decision had to be left to her. At last she had reached the point of refusing to allow him to come, as she feared that he would only open the old wound.

The time came for her last visit; two days later she would start on her journey. She had told me that before coming to me she had to pay a purely formal visit to a doctor, and she had, as a matter of fact, to obtain an introduction from the confidential physician of the sanatorium, which she had to take with her. She had not been to this doctor before, as the permit had been obtained through another channel. She kept me waiting a long time, but appeared at length; she was completely unstrung. At last I learned what had happened. The doctor had examined her, had said nothing at all, and had given her the letter. She was rather upset by his inscrutability, by the fact that he had not spoken a word to her, and when she had left him she opened the letter. And now she learned that her condition was extremely serious, as a new focus of infection had been formed in what was supposed to be the healthy lung. This completely overcame her. What prospects had she now, what became of all her plans? She was intelligent enough to know what this portended. At last she went, taking leave of me with the words: " You have shown me a piece of firm land from which I *could* manage to go on alone; but *to what purpose?* So that I can die with my eyes open? "

These words afflicted me greatly. What had happened here?

In order clearly to realize the situation we must envisage the patient's personality. She is the type of child whose mother has brought her into the world with difficulty. Through her constitutional weakness—that is, the inadequacy of her respiratory organs—she had a less favourable start in life than a healthy child. Her position in the family—the only girl—interpolated between two brothers, one of whom, the elder, the talented, hard-working, ambitious brother, was always inclined to suppress her, to keep her down, to depreciate her, while the youngest, as the baby of the family, enjoyed a privileged position—all this diminished her self-confidence, and gave rise to the feeling that simply because she was of the female sex she was of less value than the others. Further, what she saw of her parents' marriage confirmed her opinion that the woman is always at a disadvantage. The child did not feel safe and sheltered in the heart of her family. Moreover, she did not receive from her mother her first impression of human reliability, for, as we have heard, she was at first more attached to her father. That we can understand, for her mother, who is described as a fragile, sensitive person, was certainly nervous and irritable as a result of the difficulties of her marriage, so that her behaviour to the child was doubtless anything but what it should have been; while for her father, quiet, superficial, and indolent, it was easier to win the child's affection. Yet even this relation proved to be unreliable. As a result of this constellation, intensified by the pressure exerted by the elder brother, and the feeling that her parents loved him better than they loved her, the child, with her lack of self-confidence, developed a burdensome sense of inferiority. Compensation was bound to follow: but how?

This was the line to be followed: diligence, talent, intellectuality were already too far monopolized; how should she, a feeble girl, excel her brother in these? In this connexion she could only try not to fall behind him, and even that demanded a great effort. There must be something else that she could do; and her ambition egged her on. So she contrived to shake off her sense of inferiority while endeavouring to achieve perfection. Her aim was to become a human being of exceptional worth, incapable of failures and mistakes; that is, to be quite 'on top.' Over and over again she had to realize that people—that is, men—are not to be trusted. The friend, who was the object of her first, half-unconscious affection, betrayed her; he treated her in such a way that he forced her to believe that she was worthless to him. How then did it happen that she, who was always seeking for human worth, adopted such a contrary attitude in respect of sexual relations, inasmuch as she was always attracted by men who for her were out of the question? If we reflect that owing to the experiences of her early childhood she felt that the mere fact of belonging to the female sex placed her in a position of inferiority, we shall be able to understand her. She is the woman with the 'masculine protest,' who wishes to prove that she is not a weak woman but a valuable human being, and so she is spurred into engaging in the struggle for power precisely where she knows that women are lightly valued. Although she tried to establish a sexual relationship into the bargain, she did not succeed, on account of incompatibility. This too we can understand; she engages in the struggle for power, but she does not depend on this in order to 'come out on top.' Her sexuality is in correspondence with her aim! And now she meets the man who is to be her fate. She, clever and critical, does not see that this man is a crass egoist, who uses every woman as long as he needs her; a 'fanatic for truth' as he calls himself, whose life is built up on lies. She does not see this, because here for the first time she experiences what she has sought all her life: complete affirmation. She dare not see clearly, for if she did so everything would fall in ruins about her; and she would not, through loving this particular man, experience this enhancement of her sense of personality. She will never see clearly when her aim is at stake; so she did not notice that the catastrophe was brewing; and so she, with her strict love of truth, adopted a policy of camouflage when it was a question of avoiding defeat, of remaining 'on top.' That she abandoned her studies is understandable; she now derived her sense of worth from other sources. She had staked all her capital on *one* card; on her relation to this man, without regard for other possibilities and capacities; and so, if the card turned out to be a blank, complete ruin must follow. Her depression is the expression of impotent wrath; she is angry with herself, with the thought that this is happening to *her*, with the fate that has treated her so. In consequence of her discouragement she always makes herself the object of her wrath. She was not capable, when in the time of her alleged happiness she perceived her mistake, of reconstructing her life on her own responsibility. Just as when she was a little child she had been forced to submit to her brother's injustice, and as a young girl to the unreliability of her friend, so, as a conscious adult, she believed that she must submit to ill-usage. She must always be badly treated, she was condemned to suffer, to take upon herself a fraction of the world's baseness; she, who none the less had the highest ideals. In this way a martyrdom was created, which again brought with it an enhancement of her sense of personality. At the moment when, in the analysis of her husband, she came to realize that his trouble was not scoundrelism, but neurosis, the process of readjustment was set in motion. *He* was exonerated, but what happened to her? Any attempt to escape a confrontation with herself was impossible; she was already too profoundly entangled in " the iron network of individual-psychology " (Adler). There was no further possibility of evasion; she must come to realize the whole concatenation of events, and to understand that the attitude of the little child was perfectly comprehensible; but that the adult person would not have behaved as she did if she had not, on the grounds of her mistaken attitude in early childhood, overestimated opposing forces and difficulties, and underestimated her own capacities and powers. Only this realization could give her courage to embark on little undertakings, in which she succeeded, so that they at last convinced her that her 'prestige policy' was contrary to the spirit of life. Only when she had progressed so far was she able to think of reconstructing her life; only then was she willing to follow the path that led to the sanatorium. And when she has come so far, she learns that " all is in vain; I can no longer play my part in life! " When she cried out, " To what purpose? That I may die with my eyes open? " I seemed to hear the words of the poet, " Reason becomes unreason, kindness torture." Was it right to show this creature, whose attitude to life had been so supremely negative, the way back to life? Had not I enormously intensified her conflicts and her sufferings? Now that she had again begun to find some value in life, would she suffer doubly under the pitiless fate that threatened her? This is the problem that presented itself to me.

The patient entered the sanatorium. A few weeks later I received a very unsatisfactory report; she was in bed, always feverish, always depressed. Then I heard no more of her. After some eight months I received a letter from her, written from a local clinic. She told me that she had spent the last few months in utter wretchedness, until the chief physician proposed a final attempt at a possible cure: namely, an operation. Here, in this town, she had now undergone two serious operations (costal resection). The surgeons now gave her some hope; as soon as she was fit to travel she was to return to the sanatorium and continue her cure.

Some weeks later she did return thither, and she then began slowly but steadily to improve. I heard from her at intervals, and perhaps a few passages from her letters will give the reader a very good idea of her condition.

" First, quite briefly, as to my physical state. The healing process is going ahead. I must just have patience and endurance, then I may hope to be cured and capable of work. So the suffering was not in vain. As for my psychic condition, it is perhaps improving even more slowly than the physical, but, I believe I may say, all the more surely for that. By this I mean that I am finding more and more in my altered life; that the events of the last few years are beginning to fade."

Some six weeks later still she wrote that in view of the many young people there who were ill, indeed, but able to get about, the notion had occurred to her that one might found an individual-psychological fellowship, "for I know by experience how it can help one"; and she asked me to write for her a short, easily understood introduction. It is interesting to compare her inner attitude to-day with that which was illustrated by her first dream, in which she was sitting in a circle of her youthful contemporaries, all of whom were profoundly depressed; and in which she said, " How could he, who made such a brief appearance among us, plunge us all into such misery? " It was then that she made her first allusion to the community, but only in order that others might help her to bear her burden. Now she turns again to the community, sees what the individual needs, and what tasks might therefore devolve upon her.

Two months later I heard from her again:

" The book (on individual-psychology) has been a great

help here; it has been eagerly read and discussed. The sessions were always very lively and interesting; all took part in the discussions, which were very stimulating. The palpable result is that five further copies of the book have appeared here during the last few weeks. You may be satisfied with the propaganda. I must confess that I am not one of those people, of whom there is mention in the book, who are capable of helping themselves out of their troubles. One is always losing the thread. This, of course, is due to one's tendency to deceive oneself."

I now allowed some time to pass, and then I ventured to ask whether she would have any objection if sooner or later I were to analyse her case in public—a particularly interesting case, as the organic factors played so great a part in it. To this she replied:

"Now, in reply to your question, of course you can cite my case for the benefit of your audience. How does one put it? I am only too delighted to be of service to you. This, of course, as the result of increasing objectivity. A year or more ago I should have found it unendurable to allow my personal sufferings, my mental torture, to be discussed in this way. Now, at all events, I am at your disposition with my 'interesting blend.' I am only sorry that I cannot be there to hear the description of my case. Do you know why? Because all that passed in our conversations must naturally have received a personal colouring from your personal proximity, from your wish to help me. But I should like for once to hear myself discussed quite impersonally, objectively, drily and comprehensively."

When I saw the patient again after the conclusion of her cure she declared that she did not know whether she could have recovered from her serious illness without the help of individual-psychology.

And now she had a definite programme; she would go to her mother in Palestine, but first she would make a thorough study of Arabic and Hebrew. To this end she attended the Oriental training college, and after a year there she actually went to Palestine. Before she went she came to see me again. She knew very well that she would find conditions extremely difficult in Palestine; she showed me letters from her people, from which one could see what a hard struggle they were having. However, she had resolved to build up a new life for herself. "If my body holds out I am not afraid!" she said.

Many years have passed since then. For me, the problem whether, in a combination of organic and psychic troubles, in cases where the organic malady seems hopeless, so that the sufferer appears to be doomed to a premature death, the application of individual-psychology is justified, has long ceased to be a problem. On the one hand, the fact that afflictions which to-day are regarded as hopeless may perhaps, thanks to new discoveries, be susceptible of cure to-morrow, should give one the courage to resort to the individual-psychological therapy. And on the other hand, we know that in every one there are positive powers which—if they are rightly understood and brought to fruition—are capable of effecting even physical readjustments which heretofore could not have been expected. The task which individual-psychology sets itself is this: to induce people with false aims, which are inimical to life, to change their erroneous attitude to life for active and responsible co-existence and co-operation within the community, and so for an affirmative acceptance of life. This affirmative acceptance comprises reconciliation with life in all its forms and phenomena. But death also is comprised in life. Reconciliation with life means also reconciliation with death.

FINIS